I Need My Yacht by Friday!

True Tales from the Boat Repair Yard

Rod Baker

Copyright © 2016 Rod Baker

ISBN:

Also by this author
The Constant Traveller R801168

Author website
rodbakerbooks.com

Cover by Jennifer - www.acappellabooks.com

Edited by One Stop Author Services www.onestopia.com

Formatted by Sharon - http://bit.ly/2kTYkXa

This book is dedicated to the memory of my son,
Stephen Baker (1971-2009)
As my first-born, he provided me with much of the motivation
for my journey to manhood.

This book is written in appreciation of all tradespeople whose
thoughtful skill and hard work builds and supports
the physical world in which we live.

Authors Note

In this book, I wrote about boats, people, locales, and conversations as I remember them. It may not be an exact record. I changed the names and related details of some individuals to preserve their privacy.

CONTENTS

Preface

Some sixty years ago, I left the small English village in Buckinghamshire, but the skylarks' song and the crunch of horse chestnut leaves in autumn remain inside.

At the age of sixteen, I went to sea and spent five years venturing across the world's oceans, before moving to Canada. Vancouver's tall buildings and hustle of the big city amazed me. I entered the Hudson Bay store by one door, exited by another and found myself lost on an unfamiliar street. Driving in big city traffic and navigating the huge bridges spanning Burrard Inlet were grand adventures. I wished my friends back in England could see me.

Time changes everything: I grew into urban life, marriage, fatherhood, and started my own company—me, the boy who dawdled home from school picking wildflowers, became a business owner in the city.

My wife, kids, employees, and customers all depended on me, but my father had shown me the way: *Don't look back, don't quit and keep moving forward to wherever life takes you.* Thanks, Dad—it's still working.

The novelty of high-rises and crowded streets has long passed, but summer swallows and the red leaves of fall still warm my heart. I walk the trails along the shore of Howe Sound—a pleasant break from my new *moving forward*—reflecting and writing about the time when I ran a boat repair shop in North Vancouver.

Prologue

I'm in the wheelhouse when the tug slams into the submerged reef. The impact throws me forward, and I hear wood splintering as rocks tear into the planking. I run onto the foredeck with the two other crew members. We see nothing in the inky-black night, but hear an ominous hiss as the huge steel barge we are towing slices through the water towards us. It contains heavy equipment and 8000 gallons of gasoline. It's midnight, snowing and we are in the channel leading to Masset in the Haida Gwaii islands of northern British Columbia.

I've just moved to Vancouver from England to be with my girlfriend, Louise. I don't like working on the tugs because it takes me away from her, but it's the only job I can find.

I stand on the bow with one leg over the rail, ready to leap into the channel to avoid being crushed by the barge—or burned if the gasoline leaks and ignites.

The tug shudders violently as the barge rides up over the stern and, with a horrific squealing groan, crushes the aft cabin. It stops at the wheelhouse and grinds slowly back into the water. A faint smell of crunched mussels scraped off the bottom of the barge lingers in the frigid night air. Big flakes of snow continue to fall as though nothing happened.

We are plucked off the stricken tug by Haida fishermen and board a plane back to Vancouver, two days before Christmas 1968.

This will be the *last* time I go to sea. I redouble my efforts to find work ashore and land a job as an apprentice boatbuilder.

ROD BAKER

1 - Goodbye Bel-Aire Shipyard, 1975

*"Reality is the leading cause of stress
amongst those in touch with it."*
— Jane Wagner

It's December fifth, minus ten Celsius and cold as hell, building ships in North Vancouver. We shipwrights stand on pieces of plywood as we work so the steel deck doesn't suck the heat from our bodies. It's worth it: the union job pays eighteen dollars an hour, the most money I have ever earned. Due to my wonderful new wage, and another child on the way, Louise and I sold our tiny two-bedroom house in Surrey two months ago and bought a four-bedroom house in North Vancouver, close to my work.

Each time I fire the Hilti gun, there's a satisfying *ka-chunk* and a puff of acrid, grey smoke as the explosive charge fires a nail into the wood. Once I've cut the plywood bulkhead to shape, fastening it in place is easy. I space the nails eighteen inches apart. *Ka-chunk, ka-chunk*, each nail pins the wood to the steel tab to form part of the cabin wall. It's three o'clock, one hour before quitting time. I'm thinking about the Christmas presents I will buy my wife and three-year-old son—maybe some perfume for Louise and a Green Machine riding toy for Steve.

Someone comes into the cabin behind me. Before I can turn around, Ernie, the shipyard superintendent, in his white coveralls and sporting a handlebar moustache, barks out, "Baker, you are laid off as of four o'clock today." His words leave me gasping for breath. My heart starts to pound and I feel weak at the knees. *Jesus—not now, not right before Christmas!*

On that day, December 4, 1975, Ernie's announcement changed my life forever.

◇◇◇

At 4.00 p.m. the loud klaxon reverberated throughout the shipyard, signalling the day's end. The clang of building steel ships came to an

1

abrupt halt as 220 men downed tools and headed toward the time clocks. Moving like a sleepwalker, ashamed and speaking to no one, I packed my heavy toolbox out of the shipyard.

My buddy Frank saw me carrying my tools. "Hey, taking your tools home to do some work on the weekend?"

"No. Laid off," I replied, feeling worse for having said it out loud.

"Shit, you gotta be kidding me! Right before Christmas?" He grimaced and shot me a sideward glance.

"Yeah."

"Wow man, that sucks. I'm sorry."

Although Frank's sympathy helped, I still drove home in a daze. Houses, cars and trees crept by in slow motion. I reached my front gate, put the handbrake on, and sat silently on the street, wondering what to say to Louise.

The aroma of Louise's shepherd's pie greeted me as I walked through the door.

"I've lost my job," I blurted.

"What?"

"I'm laid off from work as of today."

"What are we going to do, Rod?" Her shoulders slumped and her blue eyes looked straight into mine. She was scared, which increased my panic—usually, she was calm. After a couple of hours, the panic sank into worthlessness.

What kind of breadwinner loses his job?

Buying the house two months previously had made me proud. Our new home came equipped with four bedrooms, a fireplace, basement, carport, lovely front and back yards, and it was situated in a nice neighbourhood close to schools and shops. Getting fired flipped the joy of home ownership into an economic nightmare—one I had to fix. Louise had decided to be a stay-at-home mum and stopped working two months before Steve was born. This was my problem to solve. No one was going to knock on my door and say, "Hey Rod, heard you're out of work and have a family to support, I've got a job for you."

2

I thought of my Dad. He had died when I was eighteen but left a strong impression on me of the male as a resilient provider. When I was ten, he'd lost his job as a welder halfway through having our bungalow built. Mum was five months pregnant with my twin sisters. I remember Dad's worried face. It was up to him, the head of the family, to find a solution. Sometimes we went with him for job interviews and watched him walk back to the car pursing his lips and shaking his head. Finally, after seven weeks, he found work. We were saved. Our lives could move forward. I had to do the same; it wasn't a choice. I could hear Dad's wry voice echoing from the past,

"Everything is easy if you know how."

Male code, which meant his life learning, had been acquired through making mistakes. I had no idea how to become instantly re-employed. It would be a question of trying everything, and quickly before we defaulted on the mortgage.

That evening Louise watched *All in the Family* on TV while I lay on the bed in the dark, not in the mood for Archie Bunker. Not in the mood for anything. When she came to bed, we didn't speak. There was nothing to say.

I spent Saturday morning scanning the Yellow Pages and writing down the addresses of all the boatbuilders and shipyards within driving distance. After a weekend of worry, I launched myself towards possible employers. Three or four refusals sapped my confidence, but I continued to try and sound upbeat.

"Hi, I'm a boatbuilder. Just wondered if you were hiring now or in the near future?"

"No, sorry, wrong time of year. Try again in the summer."

The summer? Even a month without wages would land us in debt. By Friday, after seven refusals, I was at the end of my list and frustrated with offering myself over and over only to be refused. Regret, self-pity, fear, and anger churned inside me like thunder in a valley unable to escape. Blaming someone, in fact anyone, would have felt much better, but no one sprang to mind—except Ernie the foreman, or maybe myself. When I started working at Bel-Aire, I worked so fast that the shop steward, Bill, pulled me aside and said I was showing everybody up and to slow down. Two weeks before I got laid off, I saw a new young helper busting his gut cleaning up the yard. Feeling helpful, I walked over to him.

"Hey, buddy, slow down. Nobody works hard here. You've gotta ease up. It's not expected. People get pissed off if you work too fast—look around you."

Bill, the shop steward, saw me talking to him and walked over to me as I headed toward the coffee truck. "What did you tell that guy?"

"Same as you told me. Just wised him up, told him to slow down, that it would upset people if he worked so fast."

Bill raised his eyebrows. "Rod, that young fella is the boss's nephew."

Having no success finding work in boatyards, I decided to try looking for construction work and drove down to Capilano Mall, where they were building a new Sears. I found the foreman.

"Looks like a pretty big job here. Need any carpenters?"

"You union?"

"No."

"No job here then, unless you know someone."

Someone in the union, or someone in management?

I felt resentful. I knew no one in either, but I was still a guy trying to feed his family. As a recent immigrant, I didn't have any connections like old school friends or relatives I could turn to.

Unions were the reason I had gone into boatbuilding. Upon immigrating to Canada a few years earlier, a friend had told me I should get into the trades. It had seemed like a good idea and I tried to get an apprenticeship as a plumber, an electrician or a carpenter, but they were all union. It was a case of 'catch twenty-two.' You couldn't get a job unless you were union, but you couldn't join the union unless you had a job. Boatbuilding was non-union and I found work as an apprentice boatbuilder.

Two weeks without wages, one week until Christmas and the mortgage was due on the first of January. I bought a Vancouver Sun

4

newspaper every day and scoured the Help Wanted columns like a man panning for gold. No nuggets of work showed up. The warmth of Christmas spirit was all around, but couldn't penetrate my cold cloak of despair.

I helped Louise and my three-year-old son, Steve, decorate the Christmas tree. His face was aglow with delight as we attached the glittery ornaments.

"Christmas is coming soon, isn't it, Daddy?

"Yes, son, pretty soon."

"Are we going to have lots of presents?"

"Yup, lots of presents."

Louise painted the living room mirror with a colourful Christmas scene as she did every year. The gifts were chosen frugally—some fruit for stocking stuffers, storybooks from us, and the grandparents supplied the larger gifts—nothing different that a child would notice. We went to my mother-in-law's as usual for Christmas dinner. Everything was the same, but different.

Our good friends Chris and Ginny asked us over for lunch on Boxing Day. They had just bought a house on a beautiful treed lot with a creek. I wasn't feeling celebratory—self-doubt and "poor me" had taken over.

"Come on, Rod. You can't mope around the house all day," Louise was right. I was becoming morose.

Our hosts provided a lovely meal despite Ginny's dissatisfaction with her outdated kitchen. Ginny wondered if I would be interested in building them a new kitchen. Would a drowning man clutch at a straw? Yes, I was *very* interested! They said I could start in two weeks—a beacon of light shining in the gloom. There would be money coming into our household for at least eight weeks.

My new job as kitchen builder started on January 15, 1976. I bought a used table saw from the Buy and Sell paper and borrowed my father-in-law's utility trailer to haul away the old kitchen and fetch materials for the new one. Instead of the eighteen dollars an hour earned at Bel-Aire, I offered my services at seven dollars an hour; I

5

couldn't risk refusal. I had never built a kitchen before, but would figure it out.

Fear adds wings to learning.

Ginny wanted a wrap-around kitchen, cabinets made of plywood, covered with white plastic laminate. I had to get the measurements exact. You can't shave plastic laminate to fit like you can wood. It was scary. There was no foreman to direct me, and no fellow workers to discuss the job—and the work was being done for friends. If I took too long, or somehow displeased them, it could sour the relationship.

At 9 p.m. on the fourth of March, Louise started having labour pains. We woke up Steve. "Mum's having the baby now. We are going to drop you off at Grandma's house."

"Oh, good. Can I have pancakes?" Grandma always made pancakes.

On the fifth of March, 1976, at 4 a.m., our healthy baby boy, Michael Rodney Wilson Baker, was born. I asked to attend the birth. "If you must," said the matron. I hadn't been allowed to attend Steve's birth, but hospital restrictions had become more favourable to fathers in the four years later.

After five hours of labour, Louise's face broke into a huge smile as our second child forged his way into our world. The nurse cleaned him up and handed me my newborn son. His blue eyes stared up at me as I rocked him slowly in my arms and inhaled the new baby scent. I looked at him with pride, but felt uneasy. He didn't know the man holding him was unemployed and bringing him home to a house he couldn't pay for.

Building Chris and Ginny's kitchen lasted longer than I thought, but came to an end a week after Mike's birth. My stomach started to churn. I was keeping my head above water, but only just. Ever helpful, Chris told me that a colleague of his, Bernie, wanted a kitchen built—another life ring floated towards me. I grabbed it with both hands.

Bernie and Sue lived in a beautiful house, located in a grove of arbutus trees, with a peek-a-boo view of the sea. Sue dreamed of a kitchen with knotty pine cabinets. I was the man to make it happen. Their old kitchen got ripped out, the trailer loaded with tongue-and-groove pine and their new kitchen started to take shape. The smell of fresh-cut wood filled the kitchen space as I fabricated the cupboards. During breaks and lunch, Sue offered me coffee and cake and we watched the highlights of the 1976 Olympics in Montreal. Nadia Comaneci got a ten—the first ever perfect score in gymnastics.

As Sue's kitchen cabinets were getting the final touches of stain, that familiar gnawing crept back into my stomach. Thank God for word of mouth: Bernie was in the insurance business and a client of his, who lived aboard a houseboat in Coal Harbour, needed some work done. His name was Tony Onley, a local artist.

Tony said that his Japanese girlfriend was moving in and he wanted to spruce up his living quarters. I upped my rate to eight dollars an hour.

"How come you charge so much?" asked Tony.

"Well, you see this captain's bed I am building for you? In ten years' time, each of the four drawers should still be working, unlike your paintings, which once painted, have no working parts but just hang on the wall." Tony frowned and gave me a strange look.

About three-quarters of the way through Tony's job, an idea I had never remotely considered was launched across my bow. I couldn't tell if it was a lifeline or a hangman's noose.

2 - Burnaby Aero Marine
"To escape fear, you have to go through it, not around."
— Richie Norton

Chris asked me to come over to his place for a chat. I thought there was a problem with the kitchen. He was a little older than me, with a ruddy complexion and blond hair; he had a deep-sea master's ticket and worked as a hovercraft pilot on the new service to Vancouver Island. We had met seven years before when we were both newly arrived immigrants to Vancouver, and roomed in the same house.

He gestured for me to sit down, poured me a beer, and explained his idea.

"Rod, I heard there's a guy selling an aluminum boat repair business in Burnaby. I was thinking maybe it would work for you.

"How do you mean, *work for me*?"

"Maybe you should buy it?"

I laughed. "Yeah—with what?"

"Borrow some money. Pay it back as the business makes a profit. He's the only guy in town repairing aluminum boats. With your boatbuilding skills, you could repair aluminum boats and wood boats as well. You're bound to make money."

I was barely keeping my head above water. The idea of borrowing money scared the crap out of me. I knew nothing about running a business. Chris opened us a second beer. At least I could be polite.

"How much does the guy want for the business?"

"Ten thousand. You could probably get him down to eight or nine, though." Eight thousand dollars was a scary fortune.

"Thanks. I'll think about it," I said to please him. "How's the kitchen?"

"Great. Ginny loves it. Bernie and Sue like their kitchen too, which proves my point: business is about pleasing customers."

He continued to rattle on about how Burnaby Aero Marine was an established business, the only one in town repairing aluminum boats, and that the work would just keep coming in, especially as I could repair wood boats as well. By the third beer, Chris's persuasiveness hadn't lessened, but I didn't want to borrow money, knew nothing about running a business, and wished he would change the subject.

When I got home, I explained Chris's idea to Louise. She agreed. "That sounds risky. You've never done anything like that before." She was right; it was too scary. I didn't have the genes or experience. No one in my family had ever been in business. My work experience as a rag baler, seaman, and boatbuilder was decidedly non-entrepreneurial.

When we were first married, we lived in "hippy" Kitsilano and drove an old, dark-green Volkswagen Bug decorated with big, hand-painted flowers. In that era and location, the word *business* had a negative connotation. The business world was about profit and exploitation, the opposite of flower-power and love. Other people ran businesses—motivated people who drove Volvos or Mustangs, were achievers, and wanted to make their mark on the world. I wasn't interested in making marks. I was happy to forget about work at the end of the day and come home to my family. As long as we had enough income for what we needed, life was just fine.

Without steady work, we didn't have enough income for what we needed. We had moved on from those days as newlyweds with our flower-painted VW bug. The constant worry of having to feed a growing family and pay a house mortgage, without a secure income, made the idea of running a business slightly less unpalatable.

"I'm really worried," said Louise. "We have a four-year-old child and a new baby. The kids are going to need food and clothing. We have to do something, Rod."

I swallowed, hating to see her worried and almost in tears. It made me cringe. I wanted her to know she had married the right guy—someone dependable, a provider, like my father. I was fed up with worrying and damned tired of being backed up against a wall. It pissed me off. I decided to grab the bull by the horns instead of being tossed by them.

I found the address in my wallet Chris had given me and decided to drive out to take a look at Burnaby Aero Marine. I knocked on the door. A guy in his sixties, with grey hair, a thick accent and a gruff manner, answered. I introduced myself and asked him about the business.

"Yah, I been running this business for ten years. It's good—pretty steady."

He was no salesman, but "pretty steady" were exactly the words I wanted to hear, like manna from heaven—the opposite of lurching from job to job. I noticed five boats in the shop. It looked like a viable business and the guy seemed solid.

"Can you show me the figures for your annual income?"

"Show me some money, I will show you figures."

I decided to have a go at trying to find some money and, if his figures looked good, make an offer. My mother-in-law, Agnes, agreed to lend me two thousand dollars. I asked two friends, Bill and John, if they wanted to be silent partners for two thousand each. I told them I had a hot business prospect and promised their money back with bank interest in two years, and a five per cent share each of future profits for three years. I just guessed at what figures might sound attractive. I was surprised when they agreed. I must have sounded convincing— the conviction of a desperate man. If I could borrow $6,000 on my word alone, maybe I was already acquiring business skills. Raising the money was good, but scary, because it paved the way for the final step.

Now a semi-skilled borrower, I made the trip back to Burnaby and approached the taciturn owner with a casual smile. I told Dick I was ready to make an offer. He showed me the books. With his labour calculated at $10 per hour, he made a net profit of $4,578 for the previous year, which sounded very promising.

"Hey, Dick, I like your business and would like to buy it for eight thousand dollars. If you provide some training and could finance $2,000 to be paid back in one year, we have a deal."

He looked me straight in the eye. He wasn't smiling. I stopped smiling. We just looked at one another eye to eye—neither blinking. After a minute, he put his hand out. "Yah, okay, we got a deal." The handshake felt electric. It pulled me into business. I was shocked, worried, and elated.

Things began to move fast. Frank, from the shipyard, agreed to finish Tony's houseboat. Louise and I met with Dick at his house in Port Moody. His living room was full of lovely European wooden furniture, which we struggled to stop our son, Steve, from clambering over. During polite coffee and cake, delivered by his silent, white-haired wife, we arranged the details of the business purchase: I would pay him $6,000 down and start work in two weeks' time. Dick would work with me for four months, show me all there was to know about riveted aluminum boat repairs, and how to run the business. Then, I would be on my own. As Louise had legible handwriting, she wrote out two copies of the agreement we had reached. We both signed and kept a copy. The deed was done—I was in business.

The lawyer I found to incorporate the company told me to decide upon a name. Dick wanted me to keep Burnaby Aero Marine, but I didn't want the word "Aero" in the name. We'd be repairing boats, not planes. After a meeting with my partners, we decided to incorporate under a new name, but not use it until my training was over, so as not to upset Dick. We didn't want a regional name like Burnaby, just in case we moved. Using my surname didn't seem like a good idea, either. "Baker Boats" sounded like marine pastries. We came up with General Boatworks Ltd—after all, General Motors and General Electric had done well and the generic name left our options open.

I opened a bank account under the new business name. The account manager asked for a business card.

Ah, yes, we would need business cards.

Louise's friend, Linda, was a graphic artist and worked with me to design General Boatworks' business card. She said the company needed a logo. We decided upon an anchor with the letters G and B either side of the stock.

GB—General Boatworks, also appropriate for Great Britain—well-known initials to attract other Brits. The nice thing about running your own business is that you can satiate your creative instincts. This particular creation proved completely worthless. In twenty years of business, no one ever commented on the logo, fellow Brit or otherwise.

I entered the world of business with strong assets—fear, hope and naivety. The fear of failure pushed me from behind, hope of a brighter financial future pulled me forwards, and naivety obscured the stresses and pitfalls of running a business.

On the first of November 1976, I arrived at my new workplace in Burnaby for my first day of work. I felt excited but concerned. I was president of my own company, yet knew nothing about business. I owned Dick's company, but was also his trainee. I claimed to be in the boat repair business, but had never repaired a single boat. I owed lots of money, which I had to generate by being successful at something I had never done before. Yes, there were contradictions, but at least I was employed.

After making me a cup of his favourite Melitta coffee, Dick introduced me to my landlords, two friendly Dutch guys, Jan and Frans. They worked in a separate unit at the front of the building. The rent was $375 per month for 800 square feet.

"You don't have to sign a lease, it's month by month," said Jan.

We shook hands. It was a relief not to have a contract. I had signed too many documents of debt recently, and each time, it seemed like I sank further into a hole.

"The rent is due today."

"Can I give you a personal cheque?" My new bank cheques haven't come through yet.

"Sure, as long as it's good."

We all laughed. I had forgotten about needing to pay rent and hoped there was enough money in my account.

"Oh, could you give me a receipt?"

My silent partner John told me to keep all the receipts and give them to his dad at the end of the year. His father was an accountant and would do our books for a hundred dollars. Remembering to ask for a receipt felt good, and I slid it in the manila envelope bought for that purpose. It was my first official step keeping records as a businessman.

The shop had a cement floor that measured twenty-five feet wide and thirty feet long, with a twelve-foot-high ceiling. There were no windows. Stark fluorescent lights hung from the ceiling, and it smelt of aluminum. It was to be my new daily workplace where Dick would train me to repair boats and how to run Burnaby Aero Marine. I resolved to be friends with Dick.

There were four riveted aluminum boats in the shop waiting to be repaired, three Starcraft and one Smokercraft. As a wooden boatbuilder, a metal boat was a new animal to me. Compared to wood, they seemed tinny and hard, but they were my future so I had to learn to love them.

3 - Riveted Aluminum Boats and Herman Goering

"Aroline built the first riveted aluminum boat in Canada,
and arguably in the world."
— Paul Fraser

The idea of using riveted aluminum as a construction material was developed by the German aircraft manufacturer, Junkers. They built the world's first all aluminum fighter plane in 1917. It was a landmark development because one hundred years later, most planes are still built from riveted aluminum.

The Canadian George Giguére was one of the first to put this aircraft technology to marine use, which provided new options for grateful boaters around the world. In 1957, his sixteen-foot Cabinaire runabout took first prize for the most innovative new idea at the Milan International Boat Show. George's company, Aroline Boat Co, built thousands of riveted aluminum boats from the 1930's until the 1990's. Big American companies like Starcraft and Lone Star followed suit. Good ideas are always copied, and aluminum boats proliferated throughout North America. A bonus for me was that Burnaby Aero Marine handled all the local warranty work for Starcraft, a large manufacturer of riveted aluminum boats in Goshen, Indiana.

The advantage of aluminum boats is their weight, or lack of it. They take less gas to push through the water, and the twelve-footers are easy to lift onto a roof rack for the weekend fisherman. The disadvantage is that they are full of rivets, which can loosen and leak with the stresses of banging through rough water or bumping along on a trailer. The larger boats, eighteen-feet and over, tend to pound in rough water due to their lack of weight and the hull shape not being streamlined at the bow. A final negative is that aluminum gets eaten away in saltwater if it comes into contact with other metals, due to a process called electrolysis. Drop a penny in the bottom of a riveted aluminum boat, add saltwater, and a year later there will be a penny-sized hole in the hull. I once had a customer who used copper antifouling paint on his brand new aluminum boat. When moored in seawater, the copper ate into his hull, causing thousands of pinholes.

15

He brought it to us because it was leaking.

"What can I do? I just bought this boat. It's only six months old and leaking badly."

"Well, sorry, but there's nothing I can think of to fix it. The copper paint created all those pinholes through electrolysis."

"Damn! The paint salesman said it would be fine." He was most unhappy that he had suddenly become the owner of an expensive sieve instead of a boat.

All riveted aluminum boats are made from five pieces of aluminum: the bottom, two sides, a V-shaped front piece called the *bow stem*, and a flat back section called the *transom*. These parts are riveted together with solid, three-sixteenths rivets. One-inch Neoprene tape and Plio-bond sealer are placed between the overlapping joints to keep the boat watertight. Stiffening ribs inside the hull help maintain the boat's shape. Two layers of three-quarter-inch plywood reinforce the transom to take the thrust of an outboard engine.

Some of the boats in the shop had been brought in because the rivets leaked; others had been torn or damaged due to impact. The first lesson Dick taught me was how to repair leaking rivets. We took the boat off the trailer, put it on blocks, and ran about six inches of water into the boat with a hose. We rolled ourselves underneath on a dolly and pummelled the hull with rubber mallets to simulate the vibration of the boat pounding through the water. Blobs of water would seep from the loose rivets, which we circled with a black felt pen, before we siphoned the water back out of the boat. The rivets were tightened up by Dick holding a pneumatic air gun on the rivet head from underneath the hull and me holding the bucking bar against the rivet, inside the hull. The air gun clattered like hell against the metal boat hull, which amplified the sound and rattled my brain. Dick's German accent, my English accent, him being hard of hearing, and both of us wearing ear protection, often worked against our being on the same rivet.

Dick's muffled voice from below, "I am on now, rivet two after the last one, but on left."

"Is that two in front of the one next to the keel?"

If we couldn't find the same rivet, we would both surface at the side of the boat, take our ear protection off, and with no obstruction to our hearing or vision, clarify which rivet was next on the hit list. They wouldn't tighten up unless we were both on the same rivet.

The rivets were easy to access on car-toppers, but on the larger boats, the floors and Styrofoam floatation had to be removed, making it a far more expensive job.

Dick showed me how to repair rips in the hull. "You cut a square hole around the rip," which he did with the jigsaw. "Then rivet a larger aluminum patch on the back of the square hole, like this." I helped him buck up the rivets. "Then cut a square piece to fit the hole you made and rivet it on the patch. I call this pillow patch method." It was a whole interesting new world from the wooden boats I had built.

At coffee breaks and lunch, I tried to learn more about the business. "Why did you call it Aero Marine?"

"Because of float planes. When they leaked, I also repaired them."

"Where did you learn to repair riveted aluminum planes?"

"I was Stuka dive-bomber mechanic in the war." He pointed with pride to a picture mounted on the wall above his desk. "I am third from right with my unit in Luftwaffe. It was big day for us. Our unit is inspected by Herman Goering. See, he is on the left, standing." Dick was smiling and seemed very proud about the picture.

Mum lived in London during the war and had mentioned Stuka dive-bombers. She said they made an awful, high-pitched screeching sound, which got louder as they hurtled down towards their targets. The Stukas had suffered heavy losses over England because they were far slower than the British Hurricanes and Spitfires. This must have meant Dick got lots of repair experience from the ones that made it back. It was disconcerting to discover Dick had been helping to send Stukas over to bomb Mum, but at least I was getting the benefit of Dick's skill acquired in repairing the RAF strafing damage. Canada was a big country and there was room for us all, especially my tutor.

I changed the subject. "How much an hour do you charge for the repairs?"

"I don't say to anyone. Just give them fixed price. It is better."

"But you can tell me how you calculate the price, as I bought the business."

"At the end."

"At the end of what?"

"At the end of four months."

I decided to keep track of the hours we worked on each boat, to help me estimate costs when Dick left. I went to an office supply store at lunch and gazed at the shelves full of foreign objects. I knew about chisels and spoke-shaves, not office supplies.

"Can I help you?" asked the female assistant.

"I need some office supplies to keep records." She waited to hear more. I didn't know more.

"Maybe a three-ring binder and some paper?"

"Three-ring binder?" Noticing my vacant look, she pulled one off the shelf and clicked the rings open and shut to show me how it worked.

"Does the paper come with the holes already in?"

"No, you need a hole-punch and maybe a stapler too?"

"Yes, probably."

On returning to work I remembered to put the office supply receipts in the manila envelope. I placed my new purchases on Dick's desk.

He looked at the new arrivals with suspicion. "What is in the bag?"

"Office supplies."

No response. I was feeling emboldened. "I'm going to bring in a table saw next week."

"For what? I never needed such a saw before."

I explained to Dick that I would be repairing wooden boats as well as riveted aluminum boats.

Dick scowled. "Will it make dust? Dust is not good."

I trod carefully. I didn't want to upset Dick, or miss business opportunities. "I will sweep up after."

Getting wooden boats into the shop would help increase business, and a table saw was a necessity for woodworking. As it was my company, I wanted to ensure that all future decisions were focused on the well-being of the business—to the best of my limited knowledge. Failures would play a valuable part in increasing my knowledge.

It was exciting to take charge and begin to put my stamp on things—well, as much as I could without alienating Dick, of course. I explained to Louise that my plan was to repair wooden boats as well as aluminum.

"That's good. That's what you have been trained in."

"Yeah, I know. I'm just not sure how to find people with wooden boats and to get their business."

"You'll think of something." Then her face lit up. "Doesn't your friend Paul's dad have a wooden boat? You could ask him if he needs any work on it."

She was right. I phoned Paul and asked him.

I was in luck. His father did have a wooden boat and had mentioned to Paul the planking needed refastening. Paul promised to tell his dad about my company. I waited a few days with no response, before a week went by. Impatient, I phoned Paul. He sounded apologetic.

"My dad said he doesn't know you and doesn't want to trust his boat to a stranger."

How disappointing. I thought having friends who knew people with boats might have been a way to get new customers. Attracting new business might be more difficult than I thought.

I NEED MY YACHT BY FRIDAY! TRUE TALES FROM THE BOAT REPAIR YARD

20

4 - Promoting the Business
"Give them quality, that's the best kind of marketing."
— Milton Hershey

I agreed with Milton. If my customers felt excited about the great service they received, I could feel proud of my company and earn a reputation for good work in the boating community. *How could I attract customers in order to give them this great service?*

Being responsible for $8,000 worth of debt, my mortgage, Dick's and my wages at eight dollars an hour, the monthly shop rent, and stationary costs, provided a great incentive to learn this skill quickly. Not having customers is called going out of business.

I handed out my business cards to everyone I met. The new cards looked great: They had a nice picture of a boat, and the GB logo in blue on a white background, with carefully chosen wording to seduce boat owners—"Repairs to Wood and Riveted Aluminum Boats."

Instead of just giving them to friends, I decided to place business cards on wood and riveted aluminum boats around the lower mainland, let them work their magic and attract multiple customers so the company could make lots of money. I distributed my cards on boats for three consecutive weekends. It felt good—like sowing seeds in fertile soil to grow my business.

Wishful thinking is reassuring until the passage of time exposes the thinking as faulty. The magic never happened. I did receive an irate call from the owner of Thunderbird Marina, telling me not to place any more business cards on the boats at his docks. I would have to come up with other ways of getting my company known.

Yellow Pages—of course, we should be in the Yellow Pages. That's what I used to find services. Melvin, the Yellow Pages guy, came out two days after I phoned. He wore a pinstripe suit, a red tie and talked quickly. Luckily, he knew what made businesses successful—it was all about "visibility." The greater the visibility, the more customers would know about my company and the bigger my business would become.

"Rod, see this ad for West Coast Fibreglass? See how big it is?

See how it stands out?" Melvin clapped me on the back to help me digest the message.

Luckily, being in the boat business, I could double my visibility by advertising under both Marine and Boat headings. As I was the sole business repairing riveted boats, he suggested advertising in the lower mainland's five regions, so all potential customers could find me.

Melvin was compelling and logical. Not to follow his enthusiastic advice felt like courting disaster. My company would remain invisible and fade into oblivion. He spent so much time helping me, I felt guilty opting for the inch-and-a half ad under Boats, instead of larger ads under both headings.

Melvin's expansive suggestions for Yellow Pages ads would have cost me the equivalent of double my monthly rent. I heard later that Yellow Pages salesmen were trained to hear customers say "No!" eleven times, before moving along to the next suggestion. Long after he left, I kept hearing Melvin's voice. "Don't you want your business to be successful, Rod?" Disregarding his suggestions planted seeds of doubt.

By January 1977, I had survived being laid off work for just over a year, built two kitchens, renovated one houseboat, paid the mortgage, fed my family, bought a business, and was learning how to repair aluminum boats. The New Year felt hopeful. We had finished repairs on two of the boats, and Dick showed me how to make a hand-written invoice on his letterhead. The repairs added up to the princely sum of $1,449 or the equivalent of four months' shop rent. It was exciting to think of money coming in from the new skills I had learned. The business was starting to pay off. I phoned both owners to let them know their boats were ready.

"Hi, Mr Dietrich. It's Burnaby Aero Marine. Your boat is ready for you to pick up."

"I don't have the money right after Christmas. Can I pay you in February?"

Somewhat stunned by his brashness, I mumbled it would be okay.

ROD BAKER

It hadn't crossed my mind that a customer would want me to repair his boat and then use me as a loan company until he could pay. It was on the tip of my tongue to say, "You can't have your boat back till the money is paid," but I didn't want to sound confrontational and realized that in January, this was not much of a threat. I hoped for better luck with the next customer.

"Hello, could I speak to Mr Johnson?"

"No, he's in Palm Springs."

"Where's that?"

"California."

"This is Burnaby Aero Marine; his boat is ready. Do you know when he'll be back?"

"I think, February."

"Could you let him know his boat has been repaired?"

"Sure, I'll tell him."

I went to visit Jan and Frans with the rent cheque for January.

"Hey, Rod, good to see you. Sit down, have a beer." It felt reassuring to have a good relationship with my landlords. Jan pulled out some notes.

"Rod, we have been thinking about this for a while. We need to raise your rent from $347 to $647 per month. We haven't raised it for the four years Dick has been here, but the way it is now, we are losing money renting at this rate." Jan pushed the piece of paper towards me. I glanced at it, too stunned to take in their carefully written calculations.

"But, that's almost double. Does the rent control board allow that?"

"There are no controls for business rent. We won't charge you the increased rate till next month though. Give you a bit of a break."

I was too stunned to say thanks for the break. I finished my beer and headed home. Being in business was a lot scarier than I had imagined. I was at the mercy of arbitrary rent hikes and dependent upon strangers having accidents to -

a) Find me

b) Trust me to repair their boats

c) Have enough money to pay me when the work was completed.

I drove home wondering which to worry about most.

"Hi, how did it go at work today?" asked Louise as I walked through the door.

I decided not to burden her about issues over which she had no control. She hadn't been keen to buy the business and already had a house and two kids to look after.

"Pretty good. We finished off a couple of boats today. I'm getting the hang of the riveted aluminum repairs. How was your day?"

"The dryer quit; could you take a look after dinner? Oh yeah, I volunteered you to be the assistant coach of Steve's soccer team. There is a meeting next Wednesday at 6 p.m. Oh, and the last thing, a guy called Barry Smith phoned about a boat repair."

I had met Barry when I was building boats at Seair Marine in Coal Harbour; he had done an insurance survey on a boat we were building. Barry was a helpful guy in his late twenties—a marine engineer who had just opened his own surveying business. When a boat owner has an insurance claim, their insurance company hires a marine surveyor to list the damage, get bids on repairs, and ensure the repairs are carried out properly.

I phoned Barry before looking at the dryer. He explained that his insurance client's wooden sailboat had been damaged and wondered if I was interested in giving him a repair estimate. Yes, I was very interested. This could be the first job to come into the shop due to my own efforts. If my estimate were successful, my silent partners would be impressed. I would be impressed.

Next day after work, I went down to Mosquito Creek where the twenty-five-foot wooden sailboat lay hauled out. The boat had been rammed by a steel sailboat and suffered impact damage to three of the upper planks amidships. It wouldn't be too hard to fix—just replace the damaged planking and patch paint the hull. I had completed my apprenticeship at McQueen's Boat Works on the banks of the Fraser River in 1973, building sixty-foot wooden powerboats, so was

24

familiar with planked vessels. However, while I knew about planking, writing a repair estimate for a marine surveyor was a new experience.

In my best writing, so Louise could read it, I estimated the hours needed to re-plank and paint the damaged area. I needed to multiply that number by the shop rate, except Dick wouldn't tell me the shop rate until "the end."

I phoned West Coast Fibreglass and found their shop rate was twenty-five dollars per hour—mine would be twenty-two. If I started out with a lower price, General Boatworks would be more competitive and get more work, maybe. I guessed the price for the mahogany planking, screws, and paint. The estimate had to look professional. I got the printer who had done the business cards to rush 100 letterheads for me.

Louise typed the estimate and I dropped it off personally at Barry's office four days later.

"Thanks for the fast service. Which boat mover are you using?" Barry asked.

"I was going to repair it at Mosquito Creek."

"It's better in your shop, more secure." I didn't know any boat movers.

"Which boat mover do you approve of, Barry?"

"Cardinal Boat Movers are reasonably priced, but use whoever you want."

I found Cardinal Boat Movers in the Yellow Pages, phoned for a price, and let Barry know the added cost. Success! Barry phoned three days later to let me know I had the job. The very first boat I'd bid on had hit pay dirt. The New Year was starting well. Business was going to be easy.

This experience showed me that building a good working relationship with marine surveyors would be a great way to increase my business. Individual boaters may only have one or two accidents in their lifetime, whereas marine surveyors working for insurance companies were involved in multiple accidents on an annual basis.

I decided to find out who all the local marine surveyors were, introduce myself and leave them a business card, although a brochure would be better. I would design a brochure with pictures of boats being repaired and information about the work we did, sometime later. Being in business was starting to be more complex than I first thought.

Another challenge was fast approaching—coaching soccer. Louise had volunteered me to coach my son's Pee Wee soccer team. It seemed less worrying than running a business, until the day before. "Is it tomorrow evening I'm supposed to coach?

"Yes, six o'clock at Westview gym. Are you excited?"

"Err, no, not excited—more like worried. Did they say what I'm supposed to do? I've never coached before."

"No, they just asked for any parent that had played soccer. I remembered you had and thought it would be nice if you coached Steve's team."

Growing up in an English village, everyone played soccer in the winter and cricket in the summer. It wasn't a choice; it was part of the season. A group of us boys kicked a ball around most evenings on the village green. Sometimes we cycled to the next village and played the kids there. There were no adults involved. We organised ourselves. It hadn't equipped me for coaching twenty years later.

I arrived at the Westview School gym and was greeted by twelve six-year-olds and their doting parents, keen to see what pearls of soccer wisdom would be imparted to their offspring. Once the ball was on the floor, the six-year-olds ran around the gym like a pack of foxhounds yelping after it while the parents watched. It was more stressful than boat repairs, where at least I operated behind closed doors. People are more concerned about their kids than their boats, usually.

After a month of lacklustre Saturday game results, it gradually dawned on me that if I wanted the six-year-olds to do something specific on game day, like passing the ball, we would need to practice that skill beforehand in the gym. Things went better after that. I decided to put my son Steve in goal and gave him extra training in our backyard. He had good co-ordination and could drop kick the ball over halfway to the other goal. Six-year-old Pee Wees played across the pitch instead of lengthways. Steve was only five, but tall; we snuck him in a year early.

As soccer was played in the winter, it became a cheerful distraction from the cold shop and reduced volume of work. It felt really rewarding to see the kids having fun and their skills improving. It was just a matter of practice. I conveyed this important concept to my six-year-old team as they sat on the parquet floor of the school gym.

"So if you want to be good soccer players when you grow up, you've gotta practice, practice, practice." Robert waved his hand. "Kick a ball with your mum, your dad, your brother, sisters, or friends. You've gotta..." Robert waved more urgently—maybe the bathroom? "Yes, Robert?"

"Coach, I don't want to be a soccer player when I grow up," explained Robert, "I wanna be a fisherman like my dad!"

I loved working with the kids and looked forward to Saturdays as a refreshing experience of seeing the world through six-year-old eyes. When we won, I felt great and enjoyed the weekend. If we lost, I brooded about what had gone wrong.

Should I have put Joel as right back instead of left back?

It helped with strategic thinking. I analysed the weak areas and tried to remedy them in practice. I was doing the same in business— learning what didn't work and trying to improve results—like being the coach of my own company. Later, if things went well and I had employees, I would be coaching the boat repair team.

I had never been in charge of anything before. Being a soccer coach was similar to running the business, except if I screwed up at business, it cost me money.

5 - My Own First Boat Repair

*"It was so risky and so scary, and yet at the same time, so beautiful.
The truth was, it shouldn't be easy to be amazing."*
— Sarah Dessen

Getting the first boat in the shop, which I had been solely responsible for, was exciting. It had been my surveyor contact, my estimate, and my letterhead design. I decided how to carry out repairs and what to say when phoning the owner. I had made business decisions which worked!

Dick and I spent forty-five minutes shuffling the aluminum boats on trailers around in the shop to make space for the sailboat. As arranged, Bob the boatmover showed up with the sailboat in tow. He jumped out of his big, blue truck and we shook hands. He was Dutch, blond, six-feet tall. He had been a taxi driver in Amsterdam before immigrating to Canada. I thought of having a coffee while he unloaded the boat, but then decided to watch. Very smoothly, he manoeuvred the sailboat so it was aligned with the shop door and started slowly backing it in. It was only a twenty-five-foot boat, but sat high on the trailer because of the full keel. As I watched the boat inching into the shop, I suddenly realized the boat's cabin might hit the top of the door opening.

"Stop, stop, it's too high," I yelled. The boat kept inching back. I ran to the front of the cab. "Stop! The boat's going to hit the top of the door frame."

Christ, was Bob deaf?

Bob jumped down from the cab and walked back to look.

"Didn't you measure the height first?"

"No, I didn't think about it."

Bob shook his head and muttered. The boat was two inches too high to fit under the door. We all stood and gazed at the problem. Dick had a faint smile on his lips. The alien wooden boat wouldn't be coming in after all.

"If I let the air out of the tires, it might just squeak under," said Bob. With deflated tires he backed the boat towards the door. I got up

29

on the sailboat and waived him slowly in. We had one-inch clearance.

"Where's your drums to support the boat?"

"I don't have any." Bob looked fed up. "I've got some blocks I can lend you but I'll need them back tomorrow. Most shops use forty-five gallon drums."

"Forty-five gallon drums?"

"Yes. The weight of a sailboat sits on the keel and you put a drum either side to support the hull. You put a couple of wedges on top of the drum so it fits the hull," explained Bob.

The next day was Saturday. Steve's soccer team played in the morning, so I arranged to meet Bob at 3 p.m. to return the blocks. I remembered that Enno's Boatworks, a former employer, always had a stack of forty-five gallon drums outside from the fibreglass resin they used. After Steve's soccer game I let Louise know about picking up the drums from Enno's.

"Can you just take them?"

"I'll pay if someone's there, if not, I'll leave a note."

I hitched up the trailer and arrived at Enno's. There were about ten drums outside, but no one around. I loaded a couple into the trailer and left a note on the door with my phone number, letting Enno know I had taken two. The thrust of business frequently pulled me out of my comfort zone.

Arriving at the shop, I rolled a barrel under each side of the boat and stood them upright, ready to replace Bob's blocks. The sailboat had been built by the owner. It had a beautifully finished white hull and a small blue cabin, which slept two people. You could tell a lot of time and attention had been poured into the boat. I had arranged to meet the owner, Mr Goodyear, when he came in on Monday to sign the work order. The boat's weight rested on her keel and the hull was kept upright by Bob's large blocks of wood either side of the hull.

Looking at the boat end-on, I decided it was resting more on the starboard side block, so I pulled out the wedge and kicked over the block supporting the port side. Turning to grab the barrel, I sensed a slight movement behind me. The boat had started to tip in my direction. I threw my right arm against the hull and the boat teetered back to rest on the starboard side block. I felt like I had been punched in the stomach. Another few inches of tipping would have put the boat past the point of no return, and I would have had to leap clear. The home-built boat was the owner's pride and joy. If it had crashed onto the cement floor, it would have been a write-off. If I hadn't sensed the tipping, it could have fallen on me and the aluminum boat next to it, in which case, we would all have been write-offs.

My heart thumped like a bass drum, while my right hand pressed hard against the hull. My chest heaved from the shock of almost being crushed. I had averted danger for the moment, but both the block and drum were out of reach. I stood for a few minutes getting my breath, thankful to have prevented disaster, wondering what to do next. My arm started to ache as it pushed against the boat. I changed arms. It was no good yelling for help, no one would hear. Unlike the shipyards and boatyards I had worked in before, working in my own shop on a Saturday meant I was alone.

After five minutes of holding the boat up and feeling helpless, I became frustrated. Noticing the shop broom lying three feet away on the floor, I stretched my foot towards it. The boat wobbled as I lessened the pressure. My foot touched the end of the broom handle and strained to pull it towards me; there was insufficient grip. Still keeping up the pressure against the hull with my right hand, I stood on one leg to pull off my left shoe and sock. I maintained pressure on the boat and slid my foot towards the broom handle, gripped it between my toes, and pulled. It hurt, but the broom moved half an inch with each pull. When it got close enough, I slipped my foot under the handle and lifted it up to my left hand. Gripping the broom shaft, I hooked the bristle end around the barrel and inched it towards me until it was within reach, then shoved the barrel under the boat and jammed a wedge on top to make it secure.

I sat on the floor in shock. My right arm trembled from the strain of pushing against the hull. I sucked in air with relief. I smoked a cigarette using my left hand while staring at the boat, made myself a coffee, and lit another cigarette. I swore out loud at the boat for a while, and I swore at myself for being so stupid. If it had fallen, it would have been the end of my new business. Next time, if there was a next time, I would put the drums under first and then pull the blocks out.

There are no lessons about how to block up a sailboat, but after that day, I was never cavalier about blocking up any boat.

It was ten after three. I phoned Bob to tell him his blocks were ready for pick-up. His wife said he was out on another job and would pick them up next week.

I struggled with whether to tell Louise about the sailboat almost falling on me. It would be nice to share, but then she may wonder what kind of moron she had married and just worry more. I gave Louise and Steve a big hug when I walked in the door and said nothing—glad to have made it home at the end of *that* day.

The sailboat owner came in on Monday. I felt nervous—like a first date.

"Hi, my name's Ron. You going to do a good job with my boat? She took me four years to build. My wife and I go out on her every weekend. She's my pride and joy."

"Yeah, don't worry; we'll fix her up like new. I did my apprenticeship building wooden boats. It should be done in a couple of weeks."

"That long? Faster would be better; we go out on her every weekend—even in the winter."

"I'll see what I can do. Could you sign here, please? It's giving us permission to do the work." Louise had typed out the estimate again, but instead of "Estimate" for the title, she had changed it to "Work Order," and put a line for the owner's signature at the bottom. Dick avoided looking at the wooden intruder—an unwanted visitor to his world of aluminum boats.

I worked on the sailboat after Dick had gone home and took care to sweep up the sawdust. Two weeks later, the work was finished, the owner approved the job and Bob loaded it back onto the trailer with flattened tires. I watched it slide narrowly back under the doorframe—the first boat I'd found, estimated, blocked-up, and repaired on my own. It had come within inches of being my last.

6 - Red Flags Fluttering The Winds of Change
"When you are through changing, you are through."
— Bruce Barton

My new role as a business owner was exciting, but challenging. Being in charge of everything was like parenting an unpredictable child. Each time I hit an unexpected snag, I got a hollow feeling in my stomach—a red flag fluttering. After six months in business, there was a parade of red flags flapping noisily inside me.

I needed a shop with a higher door to accommodate bigger boats, a lease to stop unexpected rent hikes, owners to pick up their boats and pay for them when the repairs were finished, and a brochure listing the services we provided. I had to find a way of getting materials to the shop without buying them in person; it had taken me over two hours to get the mahogany planking for the sailboat.

It would be more efficient to have accounts with suppliers so I could pay bills monthly, and a revolving bank loan would be helpful for when accounts receivable were slow coming in. One by one, I started to put these things in place, but more difficult to ensure was a constant supply of work to pay for everything.

As I became more familiar with the boating world, I realized most boats were made of fibreglass. To ensure a steady supply of work, it would be helpful if I learned how to work with polyester resin.

Business seemed to be about confronting and overcoming challenges. Once I had found solutions to all the problems, business would be plain sailing. This was the lie I invented to reassure myself that things would get easier—they didn't. I just got more used to handling the problems of running a business. Once I had found a solution, it meant that area of the business ran more efficiently, which often meant more business, which created more problems. Like maintaining a house—as soon as one part is upgraded, it highlights other parts which need doing. By the time you have gone around and fixed everything in the house, the first thing you upgraded is obsolete.

As planned, Dick left after four months. I had mixed emotions: In one way, I was happy to be finally on my own. He had been a prickly guy to deal with because of his rigid ideas. I once questioned his judgment on a repair quote. He looked me in the eye and said: "When I say it is so, then so it is." On the other hand, I was grateful. Dick had given me an excellent grounding in riveted aluminum boat repairs—useful if I could manage to remain in business.

On his last day, as we were shaking hands and saying a warm goodbye, he pulled me toward him and whispered huskily, "I charge for repairs $20 per hour. It's best if you don't say. Just give fixed price." Dick picked up his lunch box, walked out of the shop, and out of my life. The training wheels were off. I was on my own.

After Dick left, I decided to move the shop to North Vancouver, close to my home. I found a 3,000-square-foot building for rent. It had a fourteen-foot-high, twelve-foot-wide roll-up door, great for getting large boats in the shop—just what was needed to expand the business. As I was signing the three-year lease with Mike, from Mica Holdings, he looked me in the eye and commented, "So, you got lotsa money?" I didn't know why he'd said that, or how to respond, so I just smiled.

Boat repairs are fickle. You can't plan them. You wait, like a spider sensing vibrations on the web; then you run out and try to snag your next meal. My new improved web included relationships with four marine surveyors. I had found them in the Yellow Pages, gone to their offices, introduced myself, and dropped off a business card. Marine surveyors were obviously the route to success, and would bring in a lot more business. I wanted to be ready by having a larger shop. The rent was $840 per month plus "triple net"—a term new to me, which I found out meant that the occupier pays the base rent, plus the other building costs, such as utilities, insurance, and taxes on the building.

My silent partners and I moved three aluminum boats on their trailers over to the new location at 1460 Columbia Street in North Vancouver. The floor was filthy dirty with oil from the previous occupant, a trucking company. Mike offered me a week's free rent to clean up the mess. It took me two days with a huge rotary scrubbing machine and lots of detergent.

Three days after moving in, I got a call from another marine surveyor, Terry, an associate of Barry's. Terry asked me if I was interested in quoting on a twenty-eight-foot fibreglass sailboat boat belonging to Bill McGibbon. It had hit the rocks and was leaking.

Yes! The new shop was already reaping benefits.

That size sailboat would never have fitted through the door at my former location.

I had never worked on fibreglass boats before, but decided that if we got the job it would be a great incentive to learn. I drove to Granville Island Marina where the boat was hauled out, looked at the damage, and measured the height of the boat to make sure it would fit into the shop. I guessed what the labour might be, added a hundred dollars for materials and dropped the estimate off to Terry.

When working at McQueen's, George sometimes got fibreglassers in to coat the top of the wheelhouse. As wooden boatbuilders, we looked down on fibreglass as being smelly, awful stuff and were glad when the fibreglass work was finished and the shop smelled of cedar and mahogany again. I could no longer afford such a snooty attitude. Terry phoned to let me know that my bid was successful and that the owner was going to drop by the shop and sign the work order in two days' time.

Maybe the job was awarded to me because I was unfamiliar with fibreglass repairs and had bid too low. Never mind, I had other worries. If boat owners would soon be walking through the door, the shop needed to look, and be, more organised.

In my new shop, there was a small, twelve-foot by eight-foot office space on the left as you went in. Currently, the phone sat on a chair brought from home. I needed something to write estimates on and a desk where customers could sign work orders. There was nowhere to put the phone, my manila envelope full of receipts and the three ring binder. Unprepared and slightly panicky, I searched for fast solutions.

There was an abandoned house on a vacant lot next to my shop. I walked inside, knocked the pins off an interior door, and brought it

37

back to my office. I screwed one end to the wall and put a couple of two-by-fours under the other end for legs. I picked up the paperwork the new jobs had generated, along with my new office phone, and put them all on my new platform. My office was now equipped with a phone, a three ring binder, kind of a desk, and a chair to sit on. I was ready for the owner, but concerned he might ask me questions about the repair.

Bill McGibbon arrived in the shop to sign the work order. He was a short Scotsman with greying hair. He gave a long and detailed explanation about how it had been foggy and his depth sounder hadn't been working when he ran aground. I was sympathetic and kept on topic, happy to discuss running aground rather than repair details.

As soon as Bill left I scanned through the Yellow Pages and, after a few calls, found a fibreglass expert called Art who said he would help with the repairs. Next day, Art arrived at the shop. He was stocky with brown curly hair, which fell over his glasses. He had a brusque manner, which hinted that he didn't suffer fools gladly. I had to be on my toes around him. As well as hiring Art to do the job, I asked him to show me the basics of fibreglass repairs.

"You bid on the fucking boat without knowing how to repair it?" Art chuckled, but agreed to help anyway. He showed me the rolls of fibreglass he had in his truck. They were thirty-eight inches wide and came in three types—mat, made of short, criss-crossed fibres stuck together; cloth, which was woven like burlap; and roving, which was like heavy gauge cloth. Glass fibre is stronger than steel by weight, but can be cut with scissors to any size, which is handy for the repair business.

There was about a ten-inch area of impact damage where Bill's boat had hit the rocks. Art cut out some round shapes of mat and roving, about eighteen inches bigger than the impact area. Using the jigsaw, I cut out the flooring above the damaged hull.

"You gotta grind the fibreglass before the new resin will stick because there's wax on the surface of the hull."

We both put masks on. A cloud of dust went up as Art ground the hull on the inside of the impacted area. The dust had a sweet, dry smell. Art put twenty cc of catalyst in a gallon can of resin.

"Here, stir this thoroughly. You might as well do something." Art slopped resin from the freshly stirred can onto the hull and used a paint roller to wet out the area, about nine inches bigger all round than the damage. He placed some mat onto the resin, slopped more resin onto the mat, and rolled it on with a paint roller.

"You always put mat on first; its sticks like shit to a blanket."

"I see."

"The next layer is roving for strength." He laid a piece of roving over the mat and slopped on some more resin, before wetting out the roving with the paint roller.

"We're gonna lay on mat roving, mat roving, and more mat roving—six layers on the inside overlapping the damage. That's what maintains the integrity of the hull strength. You're bridging across the impacted area."

We worked together. I wetted out the layers of fibreglass with resin using the paint roller, while Art rolled out the air bubbles with a grooved steel roller. He explained that wetting out layers of fibreglass with resin was called "laminating." It was the same process used to build fibreglass hulls. It was a bit like wallpapering with multiple layers.

After the inside patch had set up, we started on the outside of the hull where the boat had hit the rocks.

"Here, you take the grinder. Grind out all that white shit that's delaminated till you get to good, solid material."

I grabbed the disc grinder and followed his instructions. We became immersed in clouds of fine white dust and I could hardly see.

"That's not bad. Make it dish-shaped and smoother around the edges. We gotta apply laminate to the area you ground out." More dust.

"Good, now we're gonna need half a gallon of resin to wet out the laminate on the outside. How many cc of catalyst you gonna put in?"

"Ten?"

"That's right. You gotta be careful. You put too much catalyst in and the resin sets up before you've finished laminating. You put way too much in and the can gets real hot and bursts into frigging flames."

"I see." I decided not to exceed twenty cc per gallon.

After the laminate had cured and got hard, Art ground it flush with the hull and faired it smooth, ready for me to apply antifouling paint.

Given that eighty-five per cent of boats were made of fibreglass, I thought the knowledge learned from Art would come in very useful— if I managed to stay in business. There was more to learn, but it was a good start.

Fibreglass was a dream material for boat owners because it looked smooth and shiny, had minimum maintenance, and was very strong. For boat repairers it was less wonderful. Grinding fibreglass produced a shop full of itchy dust which gave your skin a rash.

We used resin and asbestos fibres mixed in a five-gallon pail to make a coarse, strong putty called "bear-shit" for filling large voids. To make fine putty used for fairing, we mixed resin with fumed silica. Art said to watch out for the silica. "It's bad for your lungs." It turned out we should have been concerned about asbestos. Twenty years after I left the business, X-rays showed asbestos in my lungs.

When laminating with resin, it seemed to get on the floor, your clothes, hair, fingernails, and shoes. It had a strong, pungent, plastic odour that didn't stop at the shop door. It formed part of my children's image of me—a man who came home at the end of the day smelling like plastic. As I walked through the door after my first day working with fibreglass, Steve piped up, "Dad, you smell funny."

Louise agreed. "He's right, Rod. Maybe you could leave your clothes by the basement door so they don't smell up the house?"

7 - The Empty Shop

"Failure doesn't mean you are a failure;
it just means you haven't succeeded yet."
— Robert H Schuller

In December of 1977, I had been in business for a year. The first Concorde flight had landed in New York, and Jimmy Carter pardoned Vietnam draft dodgers. Canada changed its street signs to the metric system, but what remained unchanged was the Vancouver weather; we received the usual copious amounts of cold rain or sleet as the temperature hovered between zero and four degrees Celsius.

On the soccer front, I assured doubtful mothers who phoned to check, "Yes, we are playing today, even though it's raining," and instructed them to put garbage bags under their sons' soccer jerseys, to keep them dry. "Don't forget to make holes in the bags for the arms and head."

In the dismal weather, not many people were boating. I finished working on Bill's boat, two large aluminum boats, and two car-toppers. Nothing else came in. The 3000-square-foot shops lay empty. My new acquisition to improve business was costing me $890 per month, plus triple net of $240, yet earning nothing. I stood in the middle of the shop, the silence ringing in my ears, thinking of the boats we had repaired there. I could still see them—the shadows of their forms lingering on the shop floor.

I needed to stop daydreaming and find a project to take my mind off the lack of work. A desk—if ever a business needed a proper desk, it was General Boatworks. Now that I had time to breathe and look around, the makeshift door/desk looked rudimentary. Had I realized that Jeff Bezos would copy my idea and use doors as desks to save money when he started Amazon in 1994, I may have felt less amateurish.

Sometimes if you are lacking something, you over-compensate. The piles of paper proliferating like urban sprawl across the makeshift platform were an annoying mess. I decided to build a desk with multiple drawers to solve the problem of burgeoning paperwork once and for all.

I bought three sheets of plywood and two sheets of oak plastic laminate to make as big a desk as was practical for my office—seven-feet long by three-feet-six inches wide. The desk would have seven drawers on the front—three on either side, with one in the middle, and the same configuration on the back. I hoped, one day, that a secretary would sit opposite me. We would have seven drawers each, plenty of room to accommodate my growing business.

Maybe Louise would work with me when the kids were older?

By noon the next day, I was the proud owner of a fourteen-drawer piece of furniture. It was the desk of desks, the newest, smartest thing in the shop. Upon completion, I shovelled all papers and paraphernalia into the drawers, sat down, and admired my beautiful empty desktop. Now, I was organized. The only item visible on the pristine surface was the telephone—it rang.

"General Boatworks."

"It's Art, how's it going?"

"Good. I just built myself a brand-new desk."

"About fucking time! Listen, you busy? I gotta job in Newton I need a hand with—building a new boat. You interested?"

"Yeah, I'm interested."

"Okay, come out to Newton and I'll show you where we are going to build it. Here's the address."

I rummaged through the seven drawers in the front and then looked in the seven at the back.

Where had I put the damn notepad?

The owner of Cloverdale Paint wanted to build a forty-four foot sailboat for the Admiral's cup race in Britain. It would be balsa-core construction, and Art needed my boatbuilding knowledge to help build the hull. My heart skipped a few beats. At last, something. It wasn't in the shop, but at least some money would be coming in.

Each day I drove from North Vancouver to a former paint manufacturing warehouse in Newton—an eighty-five kilometre round trip. I earned enough to pay my mortgage and gas, with a bit left over for food. Fortunately, some receivables came in from previous repairs, so I didn't have to default on the shop lease.

Louise asked me why I had just rented the shop, but was driving to Newton every day. Good question. I explained that as we didn't have much work in the shop during winter, I was taking the opportunity to learn more about fibreglass.

"You don't have any work in the shop? That's worrying."

"Yeah it is, but less people go boating at this time of year. Things will probably pick up when the weather improves."

Building a boat hull is an ancient skill that has changed surprisingly little with time. When the Vikings built their longboats, the technique they used was to make a small wooden model, then lift the measurements from the model and expand them to construct the full-size vessel.

Modern boats start life as a small grid of numbers on paper provided by a naval architect. The numbers provide the dimensions for the boat frames, which form the skeleton of the boat.

Art and I tacked eighteen sheets of quarter-inch plywood on the floor to make a large rectangle, forty-eight-feet-long and twelve-feet-wide. I transferred the measurements from the sheet of paper onto the plywood to get the full-size lines of the boat.

The procedure is called "lofting," because it harkens back to the days when boat lines were laid out in the boatyard's loft—away from the clutter of the machinery and men working on the shop floor.

From the lines drawn on the plywood, we made the frames and placed them six feet apart, upside down on the floor, to form the skeleton of the boat. We held the frames in place by screwing two-by-fours in between them, and fastened sheets of plywood to the frames to form the skin of the boat. We had assembled the hull upside down so it would be easier to apply fibreglass. The actual boat hull would be shaped around this male mold.

Art found a couple of helpers. A forty-four-foot boat was too big a job for two of us to build. Shortly after they arrived, he instructed one of the helpers to go out for coffee and doughnuts. The guy looked surprised and started to say something.

"Helpers always get the coffee. Right?" said Art.

"But—" the guy started to argue.

Art glared at him. "But what?"

"Nothing."

The coffee and doughnuts were duly delivered.

The first step was to apply a layer of fibreglass laminate over the male mold and sand it perfectly smooth. We then sprayed on a coat of green release agent so the newly-made hull wouldn't stick to the mold.

We applied three layers of mat and cloth over the mold, wetting each layer with resin. While that laminate was still wet, we laid on the balsa core "sandwich" over the whole hull. The balsa core came in three-foot by six-foot flexible sheets—little one-inch squares of balsa wood stuck on a fabric backing.

The last stage was to lay fibreglass over the balsa core to form the outer skin of the hull. This had to be completed all at one time. We armed ourselves with paint rollers and resin. Art put a tape of classical music on his giant ghetto-blaster, and four of us, wearing white coveralls, started laying up the outer shell of the big boat to the sound of Wagner's *"Ride of the Valkyries."* We needed to get all the layers of fibreglass on before the resin started setting up, so we added less catalyst.

It took us six hours. The stirring music of *"Flight of the Bumble Bees"* and *"The Sabre Dance"* spurred us on and kept our aching arms working as we rolled resin into layer after layer. As we became weary, Art switched to *"Dancing Queen"* and other Abba hits for the last hour and a half. The cassette was running hot and the air hung heavy with resin fumes as the large racing hull received the final layer. We cleaned up our tools with acetone, peeled off our coveralls and stood back to admire our work, tired but satisfied.

The next day, everything had set up rock solid. We started the finishing process of fairing it smooth and painting it with an epoxy undercoat followed by a urethane topcoat. We carefully turned the

44

hull over so that it was the right way up, then cut out the male mold to leave the freshly formed hull.

The final product weighed so little that a man could pick up one end of the forty-four-foot hull by himself.

With the boat hull completed, my part of the boat construction was finished. Voila! Mr Vogel had his hull, I had learned about balsa core construction and painting with urethane, and my bacon had been saved by five weeks of income. I hoped 1978 would bring in more business. If it didn't, I would have to default on the lease.

8 - Getting More Organised

"If you can find a path with no obstacles;
it probably doesn't lead anywhere."
— Frank A. Clark

Just as we finished the hull on Mr Vogel's boat, I secured a big job from an estimate I had tendered to Jim, a Scots engineer who was new to the marine surveying field. My estimate was successful as I got the job, but I was still a novice at estimating.

The trick was to bid lower than the competition, but high enough to make money—an uncertain middle ground. If you got the job, you worried you had bid too low. If you didn't get the job, you worried you had bid too high. Without proficiency at this one singular skill, any yacht repairer would go broke. I bid on the lower side. It was embarrassing to have an empty boat repair shop.

The new repair challenge was an older, thirty-six-foot, carvel-planked, wooden cabin cruiser that had hit a deadhead (a semi-submerged log) in the Fraser River and sank. There was a twist to getting this job. I had bid against my former employer George Fryatt, at Bel-Aire Shipyard, and won.

The specs called for us to repair the broken planking and everything else damaged from the boat being submerged in saltwater.

I was excited about this big job; it was a $10,000 repair. Prior to this, the largest repair job I had completed was about $1,800. The owner, Mr Oliver, came in and signed the work order. He seemed like a pleasant guy and wanted to know when we would be finished. I told him six weeks. It was a guess.

"You're kidding. That long?"

"We'll try to get it done as fast as possible, but you want a good job, not a rush job, right?"

He looked perplexed, and then nodded in agreement. It was my new line—sometimes it worked.

My biggest job ever was exciting, but also worrying. I often awoke early in the morning thinking about it. Working was better than worrying. I went to the shop a few times at 5 a.m. to start removing all the debris and cleaning the oil from the interior of the new project.

Just after Bob the boat mover brought this boat into the shop, I got three more repair jobs—two twenty-foot leaking aluminum boats and a nineteen-foot fibreglass Bell Buoy runabout with bow damage. I had been bidding low due to lack of work, but two weeks later I was wondering how to cope with the sudden flood of boats.

Maybe all the bids had been too low?

I needed everything at once—more tools, fastenings, materials, and probably workers. Luckily, it wasn't high boating season so the owners weren't in a rush.

I drove to Acklands tool supply store with my father-in-law's trailer and bought an industrial $900 table saw, a skill saw, disk sander, vice, bench grinder, mini-grinder, and another electric drill to add to my growing tool collection. I was proud of my new $900 table saw. Its versatility made it the most valuable tool in the shop—necessary for precision woodwork. My old table saw was transported back to the house for home projects.

I built a big cupboard for materials and tools, and then a workbench upon which I mounted a vice and a bench grinder. To finish off, I bought a used band saw from the Buy-and-Sell. My shop was beginning to look ship-shape. I was a tradesman at heart, and having a shop full of good tools made me happy. Making business contacts and estimating jobs correctly were vital aspects of business, but if the boats were poorly repaired, the company's reputation would sink and my business would fail. Now, the shop was fully equipped with the tools to produce professional work—except you never have enough tools.

As I crammed all the new tool receipts into the bulging manila envelope, it split apart and the bills fluttered down towards the floor. A deluge of papers covered my shoes and the surrounding area. Damn. It was time to do what I had been avoiding—start an office system.

We sat eating dinner that night and I told Louise about the bag bursting open.

She looked sympathetic. "You have to buy a filing cabinet and get organized, Rod. You need to file your bills properly by date, not keep them stuffed into an envelope."

Office procedures were my weak point. I felt resentful spending time on office stuff, but it *was* my business. The next day, I went to K-mart and bought a six-drawer filing cabinet. At London Drugs, I bought fifty file folders and some pockets for them to sit in, carbon paper, and a Dymo gun for labelling, then set about inventing an office system—new and alien territory.

It would be a simple system: each boat would have its own file with the owner's name and job number written on that little tab which stuck up on top. I would put the estimate, a copy of the material receipts and a copy of the final invoice into the file. When the repair was paid, the folder would be filed numerically in the "Paid" section of the drawer. This left the unpaid files in the front of the drawer so I wouldn't forget who owed me money.

That was the customer files dealt with, now for my suppliers. The Dymo gun was fun to use. I carefully punched out the name of each supply company, stuck it on the binder spine, and filed them in alphabetical order on shelves I'd attached to the wall. A copy of each invoice was placed in the supplier's binder and paid monthly. I felt proud that the office was organised, but retained a niggling tradesman's resentment that I had spent two whole days fiddling with paperwork.

As Louise had worked in an office and suggested I get organized, I asked her to come down and inspect my efforts.

Louise had taken secretarial training and when I started the company, had shown me how to write cheques and business letters. She approved of the desk, the shelves, and the way I had organized the files, but thought the office needed cleaning.

"It's too dusty."

She was used to pristine offices unconnected to a working shop, but maybe she was right. I bought a vacuum cleaner and cleaned the office once a week—usually.

Compared to my unease about paperwork, the idea of hiring people was even more daunting. Being responsible for paperwork was one level of discomfort, but being responsible for people's lives was an entirely new level of accountability. If I hired them but ran out of work three weeks later, I would have to lay them off. Given the problems caused by own experience of being let go, I didn't want to cause that for someone else.

Repairing boats wasn't like building them—you couldn't plan ahead. Four boats in the shop seemed like too much work for one person, and, as I had found out the hard way, working alone wasn't always so safe.

To get good help meant finding the right people.

Where did you find the right people?

I had no idea.

Should I hire employees rather than contractors?

Employees would create more paperwork, but I couldn't train contractors to repair aluminum boats. Each step forward was an adventure into the unknown, like walking down a dark alley and bumping into hidden obstacles.

I had a bigger shop, more tools, a better office system, and a shop full of boats. The next step was hiring competent tradesmen to do the work. This meant calculating payroll deductions and holiday pay, trying to explain to someone else what I wanted done instead of just doing it myself, planning out a day's work for an employee, and then monitoring his work to check it was okay. I hadn't a clue how to do any of that stuff, but swept along by the surging river of business, I would learn.

9 - A Sinking Feeling

"When everything seems to be going against you,
remember, an airplane takes off against the wind, not with it."
— Henry Ford

I swallowed my worries about the vaporous nature of incoming work and hired "Old Dave." I told him it was just to repair Mr Oliver's boat, but if more work came in it could be for longer.

I had met Dave while working at Seair Marine four years previously. Most of us there were in our twenties—hence his nickname. Dave was fifty-four, six-feet-tall and had greying hair. I was half his age and it felt strange telling him what to do. He was my first employee. I couldn't have picked a better guy. Before fibreglass took over, Dave had his own company building wooden sailing dinghies. Since then, he had worked in four or five other boatyards and was an experienced shipwright.

I put him to work replacing the planking on Mr Oliver's thirty-six-foot cabin cruiser and showed him how to buck up rivets on aluminum boats while we were waiting for the planking to be delivered.

When a vessel sinks in the ocean it causes a lot of damage. Osmosis sucks the saltwater up into the wiring, corrodes electric terminals and fills the batteries, so everything electrical has to be replaced. The whole interior usually gets covered in engine oil, the woodwork is often damaged by floating objects chafing against it, and the upholstery needs replacing. Submersed engines need rebuilding and the wiring harnesses replacing, but in this case Bel-Aire would look after the engine because I didn't have a mechanic yet. I found a marine electrician to do the wiring, Rose Upholstery would replace the cushions, and we could repair the rest ourselves.

OLD DAVE CAULKING MR OLIVERS BOAT

Seven weeks after the boat came into the shop, I carefully checked over the work we had done and informed the owner that his boat was ready. Mr Oliver inspected our work thoroughly and was pleased with the result, which made me feel very proud.

In addition to the insurance work, I gave him a bill for $238 for refastening much of his hull planking, because common nails instead of boat nails had been used. Boat nails are square for a better grip, thicker, and galvanised to better withstand corrosion. On Mr Oliver's boat, the common nails had corroded where the planking met the frames. I felt good that we had found this potential disaster and fixed it.

The owner's expression darkened, "I'm not paying it."

"Why not? We did the work. Look, I saved some of the nails. They have corroded right through where the plank joins the frame. Your planks would have fallen off in a rough sea."

"I don't care, I didn't authorise it. You can't do any work on my boat without my permission."

He was right. I had been looking at the job from a tradesman's point of view. The planks were falling off due to the wrong fastenings being used.

Boatbuilder Baker had identified the problem, and, concerned for the owner's safety, had fixed it.

Businessman Baker learned a lesson.

Boatbuilder Baker wasn't running the show; the boat owner was running the show and it was Businessman Baker's job to explain the trade point of view to the owner and let him decide what to do; otherwise I could be working for nothing. The planking problems we found should have been authorised before fixing them.

From then on, in order to avoid any problems over payment or safety, I always communicated promptly and explicitly with owners when any extra work was needed. Lessons which cost you money sink in deep and fast.

Despite this minor setback, I was happy to finish my first big job and got Bob the boat mover to take the boat to Bel-Aire Shipyard. Ernie, the superintendent who had laid me off, decided to put Mr Oliver's boat in the water to "see if it would float" before they installed the rebuilt engine.

Jim, the marine surveyor, phoned me the next day.

"Hi, that boat you just repaired and sent to Bel-Aire Shipyard sank at the dock overnight."

"What? You're kidding me!"

"I wish. The owner is livid. He's talking about suing you. Ernie thinks it's a big joke, says you're incompetent and that we should never have awarded you the job. Apparently you worked there, but he laid you off? You'd better get yourself over to Bel-Aire and take a look."

I developed an instant migraine. I didn't want to be in business anymore and certainly couldn't come to grips with going to Bel-Aire, my former employers, where I was now a laughing stock.

I walked out to my car in a daze and drove slowly home. All our hard work was wasted. Seven weeks of carefully refurbishing the boat to a pristine state was destroyed. I sat outside in the car feeling completely incompetent, wondering what to say to Louise and why I had ever gone into business.

"You're home early," said Louise.

"Yeah, problems at work. The big job we had sank last night."

"What do you mean? I thought you had just repaired it."

"Yeah, me too. We launched it yesterday and it sank."

"Oh no—that's awful. Why did it sink, Rod? Did you forget something?"

"Don't know. Maybe we did." I went into the bedroom and lay comatose on the bed.

The phone rang and Louise answered.

"It's Jim."

"Take a message."

"He wants you to go to Bel-Aire Shipyard right away."

No way—the sunken boat was repelling me. I couldn't face my former employer, or Jim, or the shame of seeing my work demolished. It was bad enough to get laid off at Bel-Aire; that was beyond my control. But this was my doing, my responsibility. The reputation of my fledgling company sank along with Mr Oliver's boat. My body felt cold. I got into bed.

"Are you going down to Bel-Aire?" Louise called from the kitchen.

"No."

"But Jim said—"

"I am not going down there. Please don't keep on about it."

She was right though, I should have gone. I just couldn't handle the shame of seeing the boat wrecked again after all our hard work.

My headache worsened. Sleep evaded me. I got up, sat on the front steps of the house and looked at the lawn. I slowly drank three glasses of whisky. The lawn began to look better, smoother. I went back to bed to escape, but could hear Louise watching Archie Bunker on TV. My head still throbbed, but I cared less—about everything. The problem would still be there in the smorning, but tomorrow seemed a long way off.

I woke to the chill memory of yesterday's disaster flooding into my head. My brain function was on low as I drove slowly to work, not wanting to arrive. I walked into the office and busied myself with some minor paperwork to avoid going aboard the vessel I had so proudly shown to the owner. Now it was re-sunk, and all the surveyors in town knew we were a screw-up.

Around noon, I got another call from Jim. He sounded angry that I had not yet been aboard. I gritted my teeth, drove the three blocks to the familiar shipyard, and walked aboard. I was numb and tried to avoid looking at the soggy mess around me. There were three marine surveyors poring over the boat—tapping, prodding, and taking notes. One was from my insurance company, one for the owner's insurance, and one for Bel-Aire Shipyard.

"We're trying to find out why it sank. There's been quite a bit of new planking done," said the Bel-Aire surveyor. "That's probably the cause."

I gulped, left the boat, and went back to tell Dave what the surveyor had said.

"Let's take a look together," he suggested.

I accompanied Dave back aboard, incapable of thinking rationally, but glad he was there to carry that burden. He looked around, went to the engine space and saw a hose going down into the bilge, before and pulling it up. He called a surveyor over.

"You want to know why this boat sank? Bel-Aire never installed the engine, so this seawater cooling intake hose was disconnected below the water line in the bottom of the bilge. Overnight the boat filled up with water through this hose. Nothing to do with the planking."

Satisfied that the work he'd done wasn't at fault, Dave walked off the boat and back to the shop. The three marine surveyors looked at the hose. I looked at the hose. If the through-hull valve had been turned off before launching the boat, it wouldn't have sunk. I was stunned—stunned and happy.

The awareness of what Dave had found flooded into my brain like a warm bath. The sinking wasn't my fault. Bel-Aire Shipyard had launched the boat without installing the engine and the unattached cooling water hose had caused the sinking.

When I stepped off the boat, my drooping posture had vanished and there was a cocky spring in my step. I got a call from Jim telling me the surveyors found that a disconnected hose had caused the problem. I told him my employee had discovered the hose and informed the surveyors. Not only had we not caused the problem, we had found the reason why the boat had sunk, whereas three surveyors hadn't. General Boatworks was suddenly looking pretty damn competent.

Relieved, I phoned the owner to tell him the good news. He didn't seem interested in why it had sunk again and was angry he wouldn't be able to use it. When asked about payment, he got angrier.

"You'll get your bloody money when I get my boat back."

"But we fixed it, and you approved it, so we want to get paid," I reasoned.

"You wanted extra money from me for fixing the planking so it wouldn't sink, and now it sank anyway. What a joke you guys are." He hung up.

We didn't get paid for six months, which caused a lot of financial hardship. We had sunk a lot of time and materials into Mr Oliver's boat. Bel-Aire dragged their feet repairing the boat, and then the owner wouldn't sign the proof of loss for a couple of months. Boats are insured by policies of indemnity, which means the repairer doesn't get paid until the owner signs the proof of loss.

Three months after the sinking, I got a notice in the mail that Mr Oliver was suing me for two V-birth cushions he claimed I hadn't replaced. I was baffled. It had sunk again since we replaced everything, which didn't give much credence to the claim. Eight months later, I showed up in court to hear Mr Oliver's long, sad tale of the double boat sinking. He was impressive and had a sympathetic judge.

"Mr Baker, do you have the bills for the cushions you replaced?"

"No, Your Honour, not with me. The boat sank again after we fixed it, as Mr Oliver explained. He came and inspected the boat before we launched it and said it was fine."

"You need evidence that you replaced the cushions, which you haven't shown to this court. I find for the plaintiff, $150 for the cushions."

I was flabbergasted. I hadn't brought the receipts for the cushions because they were damaged in the second sinking and it was up to Bel-Aire to provide new cushions. It seemed so obvious I wasn't at fault. I found the whole court atmosphere very daunting. I realized later that I should probably have filed a counter-claim for the planking we hadn't been paid for.

The business journey continually tugged me into new directions I had never contemplated—office management, paperwork, hiring employees, court proceedings, and soon, towards the sticky world of polyester resin. Now Mr Oliver's boat was finished, I could turn my attention to a nineteen-foot fibreglass Bell Buoy runabout, which had just arrived in the shop with bow damage. Although trained in wood, and more recently, aluminum, if I wanted to stay busy, I needed to embrace the tidal wave which had overtaken the boating world—fibreglass.

10 - Fibreglass Boats Floating Tupperware
"I woke up in the morning and saw the world has moved on."
— Sukant Ratnakar

In 1969, the world was speeding up. *Concorde*, the world's first passenger jet to fly at double the speed of sound, took its maiden flight, while the Apollo rocket put three men on the moon. This occurred just after the tugboat I worked on sank in the Haida Gwaii islands, and I found work as a trainee boatbuilder at Enno's Boatworks.

The slow-moving boating industry was speeding up too, by abandoning its roots and using new materials. Enno had jumped on the bandwagon, and instead of the wooden boats he had learned to build in Sweden, he'd started using fibreglass. The new material was a lot faster than building boats from wood.

People had used wood for vessel construction since before Noah built the ark. In 1955, near the village of Pesse in Holland, a dugout canoe, excavated from a peat bog, proved to be ten thousand years old—testament to mankind's longstanding relationship with wooden hulls. The ships of history, Viking longboats, the Spanish Man O' War, and Nelson's *Victory* were all made of this versatile, strong material which springs voluminously from the ground.

Owners of traditional wooden vessels accepted that, like any mistress, some maintenance was required. In order to be enjoyed, your boat needed some tender loving care—sanding, painting, varnishing, repair a little rot here, replace a few screws there. It involved chatting with your neighbours as they tended their boats on summer evenings at the dock.

Typical of the pre-fibreglass era, a group of sailboat lovers in Vancouver started the Gulf Yacht Club. In the early years, half the members had built their own wooden sailboats, often in their backyards. Their love of sailing had enticed them to become craftsmen, in order to indulge their passion for saltwater adventure.

However, a couple of decades later, the ancient tradition of wooden boatbuilding was blown out of the water by a small plastic

59

newcomer. In 1942, Ray Greene, a former plastics student from Ohio, built a sailing dinghy using glass fibres held in place with polyester resin—known today as fibreglass. Ray's experimental dinghy sailed into the future as the first tiny strand to unravel, and almost completely replace, traditional boatbuilding materials.

Boaters, being a conservative bunch, took a while to adopt the new *Tupperware* boats, as detractors called them, and it wasn't until the mid-1960s that boaters began to inhale the new wonder material.

Fibreglass has excellent resistance to the harsh marine environments of saltwater and sun. Fibreglass doesn't corrode like metal or rot like wood; it is strong, easy to repair, and allows marine architects to use long, sweeping, compound curves not possible with other materials. Boatyards scrambled to cash in on this new, easy building method. Many built boats in conditions that would be laughable today, and it is testament to the strength of the material that most of them are still afloat.

Fibreglass hulls are mass-produced from female molds, which start life on the loft floor, as Art and I had done for Mr Vogel's boat. A male plug is made of wood, then covered in fibreglass and sanded perfectly smooth. A female mold is made by wrapping fibreglass around the male plug and pulling it off.

Multiple hulls can be built by laying up fiberglass into the female mold, like a mother giving birth to many children. All the hulls pulled out of the female mold will be an exact replica of the perfectly smooth, original male plug. The assembly line had arrived to usurp the ancient craft of boatbuilding, forcing many skilled hull builders to find work as cabinetmakers or house carpenters.

The magic of producing perfect hulls goes unappreciated unless like myself, as an apprentice boatbuilder, you have spent many painstaking days planing and sanding each wooden hull to get it perfectly smooth, ready for painting.

I quit working at Enno's, my first boatyard, because I didn't like the smell of fibreglass and wanted to work with wood. As an apprentice at McQueen's Boatworks, I once spent four days planing the port side of a fifty-five-foot boat smooth by myself. It helped me learn how to sharpen a plane blade properly. A dull blade took more muscle power, even with the soft red cedar hull. Every half-hour or so, I would stop, climb off the scaffold and hone the blade sharp on the carborundum stone. It gave my shoulders a break from the heavy task of pushing the plane across the hull hour after hour.

As a mere apprentice, earning $1.25 an hour, I was proud that I had completed the whole side of the hull alone. It had taken four days. The business owner, George McQueen, walked by as I was finishing.

"Hey, George, I just finished planing the whole port side of the hull by myself!"

"Good. You can move around to the starboard side next," he replied, without missing a step.

The pungent odour of steamed oak ribs and the clean, medicinal smell of freshly planed cedar exist no more. The *whack, whack* of the caulking hammer pounding oakum into the planking seams has faded into memory like the clatter of a typewriter.

All the major painstaking steps of building a hull—lofting, erecting frames, planking, planing, sanding, and painting are eliminated once a female mold has been built. Decks, wheelhouses and flying bridges, all the sectional parts of a fibreglass boat, can be fabricated using this mass-production method.

The ease of boat construction using fibreglass encouraged multiple boat manufacturing shops to spring up using the new wonder material. The thirty-two-foot Sapphire pleasure boats we'd built at Enno's had hulls half an inch thick. The laying up of the hulls could be done by semi-skilled labour, thus saving money. The problem was that all boat manufacturers were saving the same money, so the only way to stay competitive was to cut corners, which meant using less fibreglass to make thinner hulls.

K & C Thermoglass of Richmond, BC, was a local example of this explosion in boatbuilding. At its peak in the 1970s, they had two hundred workers building up to seven boats a day—an amazing achievement of mass production made possible using female molds.

My buddy, Randy, still has an early model nineteen-foot K & C runabout. It's a great hull and is three-eighths of an inch thick. By the mid-1980s, many of the runabouts being built were so thin that when they sat on a boat trailer, you could see the rollers were bending the hull. In the repair business, you could often get an idea of the age of the boat by the thickness of the hull.

The mass production of fibreglass boats, and the increase in personal wealth in the 1970's, made boating economically feasible for the many who wanted boats. Like Alice in Wonderland, everyone could have prizes. Fibreglass boats enticed a new breed of "jump in and go" boat owners into the marine playground, lessening the camaraderie forged by owning a time-consuming mistress.

However, while everybody could have boats, there was still one large flaw in the boating community: Boat ownership was unregulated. Anyone could own and operate a pleasure craft with no knowledge of the sea whatsoever, and some owners' lack of competence was a source of work for boat repairers.

11 - Boating Competence

"The sea finds out everything you did wrong."
— Francis Stokes

We North Americans are car people. We travel in safe metal boxes with rescue warranties, on smooth blacktop roads lined with gas stations and other conveniences.

Perhaps it's the trackless expanse of the ocean which attracts us to venture out in boats?

The trouble is that we bring an automobile mind-set into a world of water, where the rights of passage are miles wide, move under us, are unlit at night, have no signposts, tow trucks, or fire trucks, and can swallow us whole in a few minutes. No wonder we get into difficulty.

Not until September 2009 did the government implement safety controls. It became mandatory in Canada for pleasure boaters to possess a Pleasure Craft Operator Card. However, during the time I ran my business, a person with no experience could buy a fifty-foot boat and chug out of the marina into the ocean without knowing how to read a chart, use a flare, operate a VHF radio in case of emergency, understand running lights, or what a bilge blower was for.

The majority of boaters were competent, but in the repair business I met many who weren't—by accident. Boating offers a wide variety of scope for mishaps—sometimes due to negligence, others to misfortune, and some just made you shake your head. Many of my customers' words left an indelible impression in my mind.

1) *"There must be a notice to mariners when I dock because people gather to watch."*

Some boaters were repeat customers. Dr Thom was one of those—nice guy, but lacked boating skills and seemed unlikely to acquire them. As with most customers, our relationship started with a phone call.

"Hi, I've got a twenty-eight-foot Fiberform at Lynwood Marina. There's red and white stuff in the bilge. Is it dangerous?"

"Why don't I meet you on the boat? We can have a look together." I had a policy of giving free estimates. It was a way of meeting and forming a relationship with the owner. Most boaters felt more comfortable trusting their prize possession to someone they had met.

"Your transmission is leaking oil. That's what the red stuff is. The white stuff is where the oil has mixed with bilge water."

"My goodness, I just paid four hundred dollars to get the transmission fixed."

"Sorry to hear that, but it looks like the rear seal is leaking. If your transmission is losing oil, it needs repairing or it will burn up and be more expensive to fix later."

He looked devastated and I felt sorry for him. Outside of our field of knowledge, we are all amateurs trying to understand specialist concepts and language. It's hard to know if we are dealing with an honest tradesman, or an incompetent charlatan.

We removed the transmission and found the rear seal had been put in backwards. A few hundred dollars later, it was back in his boat in fine shape. On Monday I received another call.

"Something's wrong with that transmission you fixed, Rod."

"More red stuff?"

"No, it's kind of jumping around in the bottom of the boat."

"Jumping around?"

"Yes, you know, kind of jumping around."

"Did you hit something?"

"Not that I noticed."

"I'll come down to your boat."

Upon leaving the marina after the repair, Dr Thom had come too close to the shore, hit some rocks, and bent his propeller blades and propeller shaft; this made his transmission describe concentric circles when he put the starboard engine in gear. After about a year of continued maritime mishaps, four impact repairs due to grounding or hitting the dock, Dr Thom ceased to show up at the shop. It is my belief that he probably quit boating due to lack of enjoyment.

2) "Suddenly, there was a hell of a bang and a lot of thumping."

When Mr Brody's twenty-eight-foot, twin-engine Carver came into the shop, both stern drives were missing and twenty feet of the hull was badly scraped. Stern drives were connected to the engines and mounted on the transom to provide propulsion. I had never seen so much damage to the bottom of any boat before, or since. Small pieces of grey Volvo stern drive housings dangled from the transom, and the aft end of the hull had almost been worn through. I was curious to know what had caused such cataclysmic damage. I thought the owner would be keen to explain the full the story, but he just asked if we would be able to fix it. I replied that we could repair it, but it would be nice to know what had happened in case we missed something.

"Well, I was taking the boat up the river to my home. I was on the flying bridge and a blanket blew off the foredeck and over my head. Then there was a hell of a bang, a lot of bumping, and the boat came to a complete stop."

Mr Brody's boat must have been going flat out, because the "hell of a bang" had come when his boat hit the riverbank at full speed and careened out of the water and up the bank, knocking off both stern drives. The river was exceptionally high at the time. The surveyor said that the police thought they were attending a traffic accident involving a boat which had come off its trailer. When they arrived at the scene, they were surprised there was no trailer. The question in my mind was: What happened between when his vision was obstructed and hitting the riverbank? Was he waiting for the blanket to blow off? He never said.

A year-and-a-half after we finished the repair, I got an agitated call from Mr Brody. He wanted me to pay him $447. When I asked why, he explained his boat had become infested with rats, which had chewed the electrical wiring and caused $447 worth of damage.

"What makes you think the rats came on your boat while it was in my shop?"

"Well, I never had any problems with rats before it went to your shop."

"But it was a year and a half since the boat was here."

"Yes, and they've been chewing all that time. That's why there's so much damage."

<><><>

3) "Your goddamn boat company is responsible for wrecking our holiday."

Sometimes I got a call during a boating crisis, instead of after it had happened. Mrs Jellis had been with her husband when they first came into my shop. They needed repairs to the engines of the thirty-two-foot Uniflite cabin cruiser they had just bought from Meridian Yachts. Her husband had done all the talking at our first meeting. They had planned to go on holiday with their kids up to Desolation Sound, but one engine had been misfiring and the other hard to start. We had found and fixed the problems—at least I thought so, until I got a call that Saturday morning from Mrs Jellis, no longer a silent observer.

She let me know, in a shrill voice, how they had just spent two hours packing all the stuff down on the dock in "stupid wheelbarrows in the pouring rain" and now, as the engines wouldn't start, I was responsible for spoiling their holiday.

Her voice reached a crescendo as she yelled, "These bloody engines won't work and we paid you good money to fix them. What are you going to do about it?"

"I am sorry you're having problems. Is your husband there?"

He came on the phone and I ran through a checklist: Was the battery switch on? Was there power in the batteries? Check by blowing the horn. Did the engines make any noise when he tried to start them? Were both controls in neutral?

"What do you mean *neutral*?"

"Are both handles upright?"

"No. The kids were playing with them while we were packing the supplies down to the boat."

"Try putting them upright and starting the engines," I heard a roar as both engines surged into life.

"The engines won't start in neutral because it's a safety—" The phone went dead. The Jellis family were on their way to their holiday. Together we had solved their problem.

4) "You fixed my boat for $18,000, and now it won't start."

Mr Jenson's thirty-two-foot Uniflite had sunk and we repaired it. We rebuilt the inboard engines, installed new wiring, instruments, electronics, and headliner, replaced the upholstery, and repaired the woodwork and damage to the hull. It was a great job from a new surveyor, Ken. I didn't want Mr Jensen phoning Ken again. He had already complained that the horn we'd replaced sounded different from the original horn and that his gauges had green backlighting instead of red. Trying to forestall any further complaints, I promised Mr Jenson I would drive over personally and meet him at the dock in Coal Harbour. It was his first boat, bought with company money on the advice of his accountant.

I navigated through heavy bridge traffic, paid a premium to park on the waterfront, and met him aboard his boat. He nodded briefly as I stepped aboard. I looked for clues. The battery switch was on, as was the light switch in his cabin, but the lights were not.

"See this yellow cable? It's your shore power. It should be

plugged into the dock." Mr Jensen looked blank. I pulled the cable out of the locker and plugged it in. "It charges up your batteries." I twisted the ignition keys. Nothing.

"See, I told you. You got paid $18,000 and it won't start."

I noticed the depth sounder on the bridge giving the tiniest flicker. "Here's the problem. The depth sounder and cabin lights were on and they used up all the battery power, which is why the engines won't start."

Mr Jenson shrugged.

"It's a good idea to switch the battery off when you have finished boating, in case you have left something on." Silence. "Like at home, you switch the lights off when you leave the room? Also, plug in the shore power. That way you know your battery is topped up and ready for boating."

Mr Jenson gazed blankly at me.

"Your batteries should have enough juice in a couple of hours to start the engines. Let me know if they don't start." His silent stare bothered me.

"Is something wrong?"

"No."

I faked a smile and left. I phoned the surveyor to alert him to Mr Jensen's latest problems and my attention to them. I had a feeling Mr Jenson's powers of perception may have been compromised.

<>

5) "Thanks to General Boatworks, I almost fucking drowned."

Summer Mondays are bad for boat repairers. Customers go boating on the weekend, and any problems with repairs tended to be reported promptly Monday morning.

If a boat breaks down, you can't put the handbrake on and call a cab. A disabled vessel floats on the ocean with the owners aboard until the problem is fixed, the boat is towed to safety, or it simply drifts ashore. This can sometimes turn into a matter of life or death.

Mr Thorpe was about forty-five, short in stature, and had light stubble. He showed up at my shop, accompanied by a twenty-five-year-old woman in a red miniskirt, and towing a twenty-four-foot Reinell with his black pickup truck.

"I got ten thousand bucks to fix this boat up. I want it fixed up good. I'll come back in a month and then I'm gonna take this little lady boating."

The "little lady" nodded.

"Can you do it for ten thousand?" he asked.

I wanted to be upbeat. "It's likely we can, but I'll need to look at it first, give you an estimate, and then you'll need to sign a work order approving the work."

"I don't want to bother with all that. I just want her fixed up good. She's been sitting in a field for eight years. My buddy died, left me the boat and the ten thousand."

"Okay, but your idea of good might be to paint the hull blue, and my idea might be to rebuild the engine and install trim tabs on the transom, so we need to agree on how to spend the ten thousand. We need to be specific, so you know exactly what you're getting."

A week later, Mr Thorpe signed a work order to rebuild the engine, antifoul the bottom, replace a lot of the wiring, replace the outboard motor propeller, flush out the fuel tanks, replace the cracked windshield, replace the anchor winch, fix the broken interior cabinetry, repair some deck delamination, repair some hull damage, and cut polish the fibreglass so it looked presentable.

Six weeks later, just in time for boating season, Mr Thorpe and his lady arrived to pick up the boat and handed over ten thousand dollars in cash.

"You've fixed her all up okay?"

"I don't guarantee the whole boat, just the things we have fixed as per the work order. Other things may show up." I mentioned again the swim grid being loose and the stress cracks on the deck.

"I don't have any more money, but we don't go swimming

anyway."

Mr Thorpe's initial boating adventure went well. They launched the boat at Horseshoe Bay, filled up both gas tanks, and spent the day cruising in Howe Sound. The engine stopped due to lack of fuel and he switched to the second tank. Unknown to us all, and not included in the repairs, the in-line switch to the second tank didn't work.

Mr Thorpe became increasingly angry as the boat he had just paid ten thousand dollars to get "all fixed up" refused to start. The battery finally went flat and he had tried to start the outboard motor for some auxiliary power. It wouldn't start. He got on the swim grid alongside the outboard motor in order to get a better pull. With Mr Thorpe's weight on the swim grid and repeated jerking on the outboard, the loose swim grid broke off the transom, dropping Mr Thorpe into the water.

A strong Squamish wind had blown up and snatched the boat away as he struggled to reach his unimpressed girlfriend, now alone on the boat as it blew towards the rocks on Anvil Island. Luckily, a fellow boater pulled Mr Thorpe from the water and hooked onto his boat to stop it drifting towards the rocks.

Unfortunately, when the coastguard arrived, they further upset the drenched and angry Mr Thorpe by crashing into his boat as they tried to tow it to safety. His anger had barely abated by the time he phoned me early Monday morning at home. I hung up on him three times before he realized I was not going to tolerate his screaming and swearing at me. Louise raised her eyebrows at the language she could hear coming from the phone as I held it away from me, waiting for the noise to die down. Another company replaced the in-line switch and the damage to his starter motor. He never sued me as he threatened to on that Monday morning.

<><><>

6) "My boat's easy to spot, it's the only one
floating upside down."

Jim Poyner moored his twenty-four-foot Grew sixty yards from his waterfront home in Lions Bay. Prudent owners took their boats out during the winter to avoid damage by the powerful Squamish windstorms, which occasionally turned the waters of Howe Sound into a foaming frenzy. The surveyor had told me to contact Jim about repairing his boat. I wasn't aware of what the problem was, and remembered his reply for its cool detachment—most people were more emotional   about their boats.

I called Frank Wright from Mercury Marine to right the boat and tow it to the ramp where we could haul it out. After completing the repairs, there was some delay with the insurance money. Jim paid us $10,000 for the repair and was compensated by his insurance company later—the first time an owner had ever done that. Jim was a great guy and became our company's lawyer. He was a competent boater, but just left it too late to haul his boat out before the winter storm roared up Howe Sound and flipped his boat over.

Boats are held in the sea's close embrace, which, like any intimate relationship, has the ability to offer both pleasure and pain. Those captains who take the time to respect and understand their mistress' needs will suffer less during her unpredictable moods. My business was often called upon to repair boat damage from a punishing tryst. The sea never got hurt.

12 – Subcontractors
"Love all, trust a few, do wrong to none."
— William Shakespeare

After making a few mistakes, I learned to agree with Shakespeare. It made good business sense. If I did wrong to none, it was the easiest way of not making enemies. Business was so consuming that I had no energy for enemies. Loving all was the best option; it meant treating people how I would like to be treated. It was the easiest to figure out. I learned to hire sub-contractors the same way I learned most things in business, by experience—a euphemism for learning from your mistakes.

The first engine contractor I used was Angus, the Scottish father of one of the lads I coached on Steve's soccer team. Naturally, I trusted him—he was a fellow Brit and a soccer dad. Angus told me the diesel engine on a thirty-eight-foot pleasure boat we were repairing on an insurance claim would cost $2,700 and take three weeks. It took six weeks and cost $3,800.

I was shocked, and it damaged my relationship with the surveyor. It didn't matter to him that it was due to poor estimating by the engine rebuilder. I had chosen the engine rebuilder, so I was responsible for the unexpected price hike—which was true. I was too trusting in the beginning, but quickly learnt from the disappointment of broken expectations.

In my dual role as worker/manager, I became adept at sprinting the length of the shop to get the phone. Every phone call was a possible job. However, things changed when I started to dabble in fibreglass; once catalyst is added to polyester resin it sets up—you can't outrun a chemical reaction. Sometimes I had resin on my hands and felt my skin tightening as I tried to get off the phone with a customer who was making a particularly important point about his boat.

I would peel the thin veneer of hardened resin off my hands as I walked back to the job to find the resin had set up in the can. I could handle answering the phone while working with wood or riveted aluminum, but not fibreglass. I decided to try subcontracting out the fibreglass work. I didn't feel I knew enough yet to direct an employee in fibreglass repairs, or that there would be enough work to keep an employee busy.

To repair the nineteen-foot Bell Buoy which came into the shop after Mr Oliver's boat, I phoned Art, but he was busy. Eddy, of Eddy's Fiberglass, came recommended by a marine surveyor. He was about thirty-five, wore white coveralls, a baseball cap, and carried a pad of paper. He looked at the hull damage from the outside. He didn't climb inside to check out the interior layout.

"How much to repair it?"

"Two hundred and fifty bucks, including materials."

He wrote the sum down on his pad and handed it to me. I was happy. I had estimated $450. This was going to be easy money.

"You going to repair inside and outside?"

"No, just outside. Grind away the damage. Put a heat lamp on it. Repair it with epoxy resin. Twice as strong as polyester and sticks to damp material."

"I thought you had to laminate inside and outside the damage to make it structurally sound."

Eddy laughed. "Well, whoever told you that bullshit musta made a lot of money out of you, buddy." He laughed some more, as if to hammer home his point.

"You sure it's gonna work just laminating the outside? It's guaranteed, right?"

"That's what I said, didn't I?" said Eddy, raising his voice and fixing me with a stare.

I gave him the go-ahead. He came the next day for an hour, then the next day for two hours, and finished up by painting the antifouling over the repair. I had run out of company cheques and he agreed to come back in three days to get paid.

The owner showed up to get the boat, happy it was ready so quickly. He inspected it for a while as I took a phone call in the office.

"There's water leaking from the hull where the impact was."

"I don't think so."

"Come and look."

I excused myself from the call and followed him. A small drop of water had formed on the vee of the bow where the impact had been. He wiped it away with his forefinger and another formed. The trust evaporated from his eyes and was replaced by a hard stare. He had given me his beloved boat to repair and I had betrayed his trust. Once an owner loses confidence in you, it's over. He will never bring his boat back to you, and moreover, will often tell all his friends how incompetent you are.

"I'm sorry. You are right. There are a couple of drops of water there. I will fix it myself. Give me a few days and it will be repaired properly. Forget the $100 deductible as a small compensation for your wasted journey today."

"Okay, but I expected it done right the first time. The surveyor recommended you. And it has to be fixed in two days for sure. I need it for a fishing trip."

When I arrived home that night, I explained to Louise what had happened and how humiliating it felt to have the customer find water dripping out of a boat we had just repaired.

"What will you do? How can you find someone that fast?"

"Good question—there's no one that can start tomorrow."

"Goodness! Can you repair it yourself?"

"I did a repair with Art once and I've done a little work with fiberglass. Maybe I'll try."

Next day I tried to replicate all the steps Art and I had done when repairing Bill McGibbon's sailboat—removing the flooring, grinding and laminating the hull inside and outside, then coating the repair with matching antifouling paint. It seemed to work fine, but that experience taught me two important lessons: In future I would tell the contractor what I wanted done, not vice versa; and second, all repairs needed to be thoroughly inspected for quality *before* telling the owner to pick up his boat.

Eddy came to pick up his cheque as I was finishing working on the Bell Buoy. I told him about the leak, the embarrassment it caused me, and that I wasn't paying him. He got abusive, called my company a "fucking Mickey-Mouse operation," and stormed out of the shop, slamming the door violently.

Next morning as I parked my car, I noticed that a gallon of white gelcoat had been thrown all over my driveway and onto the roll-up door. I suddenly realized how vulnerable my business was. I was there eight hours a day, which meant it was vacant and unattended with all my equipment, and my customers' boats, for sixteen hours a day. I repainted the door but never did quite get all the white resin off the driveway. It served as a reminder of my vulnerability and that it might be better to pay people lest they strike back.

Seeing the gel coat on the driveway and successfully fixing the boat myself, somehow gave me the confidence to hire an employee for future fibreglass repairs. As most boat hulls were made of this material, it made sense to have an in-house employee for this kind of work.

After a while, I grew better at selecting subcontractors. As the general contractor, subcontractors' skilled abilities enhanced the reputation of my company, because I got the credit for their work and their good pricing helped me tender competitive estimates.

After using two or three overpriced, average-quality canvas top suppliers, I found Fred from M & M Canvas. Fred made all my canvas boat tops for seventeen years.

He was a slightly built, affable German who had fled post-war Germany in 1954 to start afresh in Canada.

"We came out west but couldn't find work, so we rode the train to the Yukon. We lived in a tent and caught fish to eat. It was good until winter came," he chuckled. "We never knew it could get so cold."

Fred and his son Roy installed over sixty wonderfully made canvas tops on my customers' boats. A slick-fitting canvas top can really make a boat look sharp. Fred and Roy would drop by in their white Ford van, take initial measurements, and then come by a couple of weeks later to install the canvas on the boat. Due to his workload, he was usually a couple of days late. On one rush job he did for us, I figured he must have worked Saturday and Sunday to get the job done.

"I really appreciate this, Fred—working the weekend to finish the job on time."

"We often work seven days a week, Roddy. I figured out a long time ago that there is nothing much in life except work. So if you don't like your work, you're kind of screwed, yah?"

Other items that gave a great finishing touch were welded stainless steel bow and stern rails. For these, I used Eddie, from Irion Machine Shop in Coquitlam.

He usually arrived a little later than planned. His way of calculating how to shape the complex curves of the rails baffled me; I always watched. He walked around the boat for a few minutes, looking at the deck configuration and muttering to himself. After writing down a few measurements on the back of a cigarette packet, he nodded to himself, smiled and left. Three weeks later, he delivered a beautifully welded and polished stainless steel rail, which always fitted the boat perfectly.

We often replaced corroded fuel tanks, which meant a visit to Coast Coppersmiths on Powell Street. Entering Coast Coppersmiths shop was like going back in time to the Industrial Revolution. To get to John the owner's tiny upstairs office, I first had to locate the hidden stairway in the back corner of the shop. On my first visit there, it felt like walking into Dante's Inferno with the clanging of men pounding metal, the floor littered with debris, and the searing, blue flashes of the arc welding flickering through the acrid smoke.

I couldn't find John's office, or understand the Finnish accents of the workers telling me where it was. I persevered and found the narrow staircase hidden behind the furnace ducts. I bought over forty custom-built fuel tanks from John. They never leaked, were made of thick material, built on time, and cost ten percent less than other tanks.

Whenever I walked into his ramshackle office, John always greeted me with a big smile.

"You want tea, Rod?"

John was in his mid-seventies with white, wispy hair. His desk was a jumble of paper and strange pieces of metal. An ancient black, rotary phone sat on one corner. I drank tea, gave John the measurements, and one week later, dropped by to pick up the tank. I used cartage companies like Ace Courier for picking up materials, but I wanted to hand John a cheque personally to show my appreciation for his timely work. John was never late, built great tanks, and always had good tea.

MY FUEL TANK BUILDER

Engines are the heartbeat of a boat. People go boating to get someplace. Firing up an engine and putting it into forward gear starts each trip. Putting the engine into reverse acts as the brake once you arrive. Failure of either function always brought phone calls.

Inboard marine engines live in a stressful environment at the bottom of the boat. They are constantly submersed in saltwater vapour, and are always pulling uphill—no coasting or slacking-off downhill for the boat engine. Having access to an expert marine mechanic is an invaluable asset.

For engine work, I used Trevor from North Shore Engines, before I got my own mechanic. Even after that, we'd still use Trevor for machining and re-boring the engines. Trevor knew engines inside-out, plus he was a genuinely nice guy who would go overboard to help solve any problems. If I was in trouble with a customer's engine, he would sense my concern and often come the same day. In the boating world, reliable engine work can't be overvalued. No one buys a boat without planning to leave the dock, and even sailboats need to motor in and out of the marina or use their engine when the wind stops blowing.

Trevor's shop was four blocks from mine. We would sometimes meet after work on Fridays in the Lynwood Inn and share boat repair stories over a couple of beers. It was good to chat with another business owner. We would often talk about our problems with troublesome customers.

"I've got a big Swedish guy's boat in my shop—a Grady White," said Trevor. "The guy's driving me crazy. He comes and watches my guy working and tells him what to do."

"I had that guy too, Trev. Always told me how I should fix his boat, then he started telling my guys they should be working faster." The local boating world was a small one. It was good to keep in touch and learn that I was not the only one with problems.

One of the joys of business was to work with competent subcontractors. They were fellow tradespeople who, like me, had decided to use their skills to open their own business.

Unlike my employees or customers, I shared with them the daily stresses of running a business—having too much or too little work, meeting the bi-weekly employee payroll, customers who welched on paying, employees screwing up, stealing, or going missing, dealing with accountants, bankers, bookkeepers, sales people, Revenue Canada, and despite the wear and tear of all these pressures, consistently turning out top-class work. I felt a strong kinship towards them. They were my brothers-in-arms, there when I asked for help— unlike salespeople, who walked into my shop at their own convenience rather than at mine.

13 – Salespeople and the Amazing Office Tool
"Business is like riding a bicycle.
Either you keep moving or you fall down."
— Frank Lloyd Wright

I sensed a large vehicle pulling into my driveway, looked up from my paperwork, and saw the big Snap-on tool truck parking outside again. The truck was a giant billboard for the Snap-on tool company, an entity awarded shamanic reverence among mechanics—members of the wrench-puller's cult.

I could feel my bile rising. Ten minutes, that's all, and then I'd go and nicely suggest that the guy leave. The time-conscious, *who's paying for this?* side of me resented the Snap-on guy spending time with my mechanic. What the hell did they talk about? The Snap-on guy came every other Monday, marched through the door and headed upstairs to the engine shop for a mechanical pow-wow. I once timed him, and, after fifty minutes, walked in on them.

"Hi guys, excuse me for interrupting, but I'm having trouble figuring out which customer I should charge this time to?"

"A mechanic's gotta have good tools, boss. Gets the job done faster," said the glib Mr Snap-on.

"Well, it would have to be a pretty darned good tool to make up for the hour you just cost me by talking to my mechanic. Maybe you can show me which tool that is, exactly?"

Mr Snap-on smiled. "Ha, I can see you're on good form today, boss. Well, better be going now. See ya both in a couple of weeks."

Damned cheek. I should ban him from coming to the shop.

As a tradesman myself, I appreciated the value of good tools. They were extensions of my hands in shaping the wood to the plan in my head. As an apprentice, each new addition to my toolbox helped me perform my craft better and legitimised my journey to become a tradesman. Every other payday, I would proudly buy myself a new tool. At McQueen's Boatworks, we talked about tools a lot and envied Herman the German's amazing Ulmia tools. We talked him into getting them sent from Germany for us. I still have six Ulmia

Chisels and a plane, with a Lignum-Vitae sole, in my workshop at home.

I got the importance of tools, but not of talking about them ad infinitum on my time.

In general, I had little tolerance for salespeople coming into my shop and telling me what I needed to buy from them. As I made my living doing this work, there was little they could tell me that was useful. I would be polite, listen, thank them, and not buy anything—except for Edouard.

He was about my age, sported smart hair and a yellow ascot. He breezed in one morning and lit up the office with his smile. He had an alert manner, was interested in what we did, and marvelled at how we could refurbish even the most broken boats. He was a motorcycle enthusiast like me. He was French, from Nice; we chatted in French for a while. It was a fun hour and took my mind off work, back to younger times when I drove a motorbike with my buddies and went to France often.

When Edouard left, I noticed a five-gallon pail of some yellow liquid I had paid $300 for sitting on the floor in my office. I couldn't remember what it was supposed to do. Somehow it didn't matter, because I had spent a great hour with Edouard.

We became friends, played badminton, went camping, rode our motorcycles together, and often shared a few beers. Louise wondered if he was gay, because his BMW was pink.

"No, he's married, he just likes the colour pink."

Ed often dropped by the shop for a coffee and to give me samples of new items he was selling. One day he complained, "I give you all these free products, but you never tell me if they're useful."

Now was my chance to pay him back for the expensive yellow stuff. "Ed, those samples you give us, we pour them all into one large container, mix it fifty-fifty with diesel and then we use if for everything. It's really great!"

"You bastard. I am never giving you anything free again."

We are still in touch. Ed moved south and started a huge food enterprise in the US. He recently retired and spends time in Florida and France. I miss him.

In June of 1987, two saleswomen walked into my office. The talkative one wore high heels, a short black skirt and a low red blouse. The other lady wore black pants and a mauve sweater.

"Hi, are you looking for somebody?" I asked. We didn't get many women in the shop.

"Yes. If you are the boss, we're looking for you. We are here to help you grow your business. I'm Sally; this is Jane." We shook hands awkwardly.

I was really busy trying to get an estimate finished and didn't want to be rude, especially to women, but whatever they were selling, I didn't need it.

"You got a pretty ancient office here," Sally chortled, and Jane nodded. "Old-fashioned phone, small calculator, dowdy curtains, even a typewriter. How's business, Rod?" She smiled and tapped me on the butt.

At which sales seminar did she learn that technique?

I imagined what would happen if I patted a female customer on the bum. It did get my attention, though. I stepped back out of reach.

"How can I help you ... ladies?"

"As I said, we're here to help you, Rod. You probably haven't heard of a fax machine before, but it's gonna transform your business. We got great deals on them, almost new, left over from Expo 86, only $300 a pop. Jane, fetch one in for Rod."

Fax machines were amazing. I had used one three weeks previously to send a drawing down to Pompano Beach, Florida, but didn't know what I would need one for. Jane struggled to bring it in. It was huge. Luckily, I had a giant desk to match. Sally was a fast talker—a non-stop talker. She manoeuvred around to me again, but I stepped out of reach.

"So, you see Rod, *blah, blah, blah.*"

I was getting sick and tired of her chatter, though the machine did look good on my desk and made the office look more up to date.

"Sally, if it's used I'll give you $275 for it. Just say yes or no. I'm really busy and have to get a big estimate out before noon." That's how I came to own a fax machine.

The large machine sat on my desk for six months. I didn't know anybody to fax; none of my colleagues had fax machines. One day a guy walked into my office needing an estimate for an eighteen-foot K & C runabout that had been hit by another boat. I inspected the damage, made some notes, and typed out an estimate.

"Thanks," said the customer. "My insurance company is Canadian Shield in Calgary. I'll mail it to them and see what they say."

"Sure, let me know," he said and walked out of the shop. I glanced at the fax machine on my desk.

"Hey, wait up," I yelled. "Do you have their phone number?

"Sure, it's on my policy. Why?"

"Maybe I can fax them the estimate." I pointed with pride to the large machine sitting on my desk. "This is a fax. You can send pictures and writing over the phone line."

"Really? A fax machine. Never heard of that before."

"Yeah, it's the latest thing. Got to keep the office up to date if you're in business."

I phoned his insurance company. Yes, they did have a fax machine. I dialled the number, fed the paper carefully into the fax, and waited. The machine grabbed it and magically sent the contents all the way to Calgary through the phone line. I was impressed. The customer was impressed. Canadian Shield must have been impressed, because fifteen minutes later, the phone rang. "Mr Baker, we would like you to proceed with the repair of Mr Hodgson's eighteen-foot boat as per your faxed estimate."

Five days later, a new customer walked into the shop.

"My insurance company is Canadian Shield. I ran into the dock and they said you could fax them a repair estimate."

"Sure. Where's your boat?"

"It's on a trailer outside."

For the next three years, I believe I got much of Canadian Shield's business in the lower mainland, until other boatyards caught on. For once, Sally the saleslady had been right. It did transform my business. I never mentioned this to other boat repairers.

The amazing fax machine helped in other ways: it created factual records in my dealings with customers. It became the new best tool in my office toolbox. It meant less running back and forth to customers in that all communications were recorded and signed for. I developed a document that listed materials and labour, plus the terms and conditions of the repairs. I used it for estimates, work orders and invoices.

Estimates were faxed to customers' offices, followed by work orders and finally, invoices. It was sure-fire instant communication. Every detail was written down and instantly received. There were no more "I thought you meant that you were going to—" or "I never signed for that," or "I didn't get the bill yet."

Two years after red-blouse Sally sold me the fax machine, a later-model sales lady, slim, tall, and wearing a black pantsuit, breezed into my office. She laughed outright at my huge fax machine.

"Ha ha, see that thing, Rod? It's a dinosaur. I have just the thing here for you. It's a phone and a fax together, half the size of that thing taking up all that space on your desk. It's yours for only $900. Don't even think of going to Walmart for one of their cheap models."

Of her sales pitch I only heard one thing—Walmart. When she left, I phoned Walmart. Yes, they had fax machines. I drove there and bought a combined phone/fax machine for $340. I still had it eight years later when I sold the business. It was the single most useful piece of office equipment I ever owned.

After customers, subcontractors, and salespeople who wandered in, employees were the final category of people I dealt with when running a business. Unlike those others, I saw employees every day. It was up to me to train them, encourage them, structure their workday, and ensure their work was competent. If you have to see someone every day, you had better make sure they don't drive you crazy. Of course, you don't know that until you've worked with them for a few weeks.

14 - Growing The Business—Hiring Staff
"We recruit for attitude and train for skill."
--Atul Gawande

I wanted to grow the business, but it frequently felt like the business wanted to grow me. Either way, we grew together in a grand experiment. I practiced alchemy using General Boatworks as the test tube for my experiments. I observed weak elements, added something new to the mix and observed the outcome. Success was measured in business gold.

Melvin, the Yellow Pages guy, had been right—visibility was important, though rather than bankrupt the company buying all the Yellow Pages advertising he'd suggested, I continued experimenting in other methods.

I started taking marine surveyors to lunch. I let them know we were a one-stop shop and would handle all aspects of the repair—wiring, mechanical, fibreglass, wood, and riveted aluminum—so they didn't have to deal with three or four contractors. If any problems occurred, the accountability was all under one roof. They seemed to like that idea and it saved them shopping around and dealing with two or three businesses for one insurance claim.

At Christmas time I mailed marine surveyors calendars so they would have a General Boatworks' reminder in their office all year round. For those who had given me business, I dropped off a bottle of whisky and a calendar in person.

I had a couple of large signs made and fastened them to pilings in Lynwood Marina, a few hundred yards from my shop, so boaters could see them as they left and returned from their moorings. Finally, I had a four-by-six-foot sign for the street erected outside my shop, which could be seen half a block away. My efforts worked. We became more visible and got so much work that I had to cross the next frontier and become an employer.

Apart from hiring "Old Dave" for a short time, I had never been an employer. Finding, interviewing, hiring, and training employees provided a deep test tube for experiments. Hiring subcontractors was renting a short-term skill. Hiring employees felt like owning them; they would depend on the wages I provided for their daily bread, their dreams, their mortgages, and their family's sustenance—scary.

Where could I find potential workers?

Newspaper ads were one way, Canada Manpower another. I needed to attract the best people possible, so they would enhance my company's image by doing great work. There were problems with finding the best people: I couldn't promise them long-term employment, the work environment in the shop had itchy fibreglass dust on all the flat surfaces, and the air was heavy with the pervasive odour of polyester resin. The shop was too big to heat well in the winter and often got too hot in the summer.

Unlike boat building, there is no apprenticeship for boat repairs, so there were no papers of competency for me to examine. Job interviews lasted a few minutes. I didn't know what to ask. Even if I posed great questions and got good answers, I knew their work would reveal far more than an interview. I told potential employees they would be on a week's trial. Applicants who remained interested and appeared knowledgeable were hired.

Having employees created more of my Achilles heel—paperwork. Each employee needed their wages calculated and income tax paid. Canada Pension Plan and Workers Compensation had to be deducted, and an annual T4 produced.

Our accountant, John's dad, told me to hire someone to do payroll and bookkeeping. Donna worked at the Ice Machine business behind us and offered to do my biweekly payroll and book-keeping once a week. She sat across from me at my fourteen-drawer desk, and, on bookkeeping days, asked questions about receipts. I had kept most of them, somewhere.

Never having hired employees before, I treated them like friends. I went dirt biking with them and sometimes we skied together. We all had coffee and lunch sitting at a table in the shop—my daily way of keeping connected with my staff. When they did a good job, I let them know.

"Thanks, Bob, you did a good job. Mr Rogers was very happy with his boat."

Saying thank you cost nothing and made the employee keen to earn more appreciation.

In the beginning, I needed to hire workers who had a good knowledge of fibreglass skills, but were flexible enough to learn multiple other tasks that boat repairs required. I hired the best people I could, and often learned from them. Gradually, I acquired the sum of their knowledge—useful for training new staff. I found a person's willingness to learn and help mattered more than what they knew. If they couldn't do a good job, we tried to figure out why and make corrections, or I moved them on to something easier. If that didn't work, I laid them off.

Laying off employees was the most stressful part of business. I never got used to it. I worried about finding the right time and words before I laid them off and felt guilty seeing their disappointed faces.

There was one important repair challenge that needed skilled employees and took a long time to perfect. Much of the damage that came into the shop was from boaters crashing into things. Getting the structural strength back and making the hull repair perfectly smooth was no problem. If the damage was below the water line, we just coated the repair with antifouling paint to match the rest of the bottom—easy. When the damage was above the waterline, getting an exact match for the hull colour was a problem.

"How come the patch doesn't match the rest of the hull?"

This became an all too frequent, unsettling customer question and one which demanded a solution.

In the early days, I matched the hull colour using a spray can of automotive paint, getting the colour as close as I could. It never looked perfect. I needed a way to match the existing finish and colour so the repaired area didn't show.

I bought a selection of pigments and kept adding them to a small mix of white gelcoat until I had an exact match. Not always easy—the longer the hull was exposed to sunlight, the more it faded. Even white fades, and there are at least twenty shades of white. I put the final colour match in a miniature sprayer, thinned it with acetone so it would pass through the spray nozzle, added catalyst, and sprayed a thick coat over the repaired area. We sanded it smooth with 220 grit wet-and-dry sandpaper and cut-polished the sprayed area to make it glossy like the rest of the hull. I had found the solution!

It takes two minutes to explain, up to forty-five minutes to match the colour, and took over two years to figure out. I became proficient at this skill, possibly due to talent, but more likely driven by the desire to avoid customer complaints.

I felt proud when customers said, "That's great. I can't even see where the repair was."

Over the twenty years and multiple employees, only Bob and Kevin learned this skill competently. Luckily, they were both with me for a long time.

Don was a twenty-eight-year-old blond Australian who claimed he could match gelcoat. I paid him a decent wage, because it would save me leaving the office to match the gelcoat on boats outside the shop. After looking at his work, I saw the colour was way off. I waited till Friday, a couple of hours before quitting time.

"Don, sorry, got to lay you off. You said you could match gel coat but the three times you tried, it wasn't even close and I had to fix it myself."

To my surprise and horror, he started crying and said, "What am I going to tell my wife?"

I cringed. I wasn't expecting tears and felt horrible. I knew it felt awful to be fired. I capitulated and hired him back at a lesser rate. I would train him in colour matching. I had to let him go again three weeks later. He couldn't get it. I'd been right the first time.

Employees ebbed and flowed with the seasons. As the weather warmed and spring started snatching days from summer, the phone started ringing.

"Hi, Rod. Gotta get my boat fixed—transom's rotten. When's a good time to bring it in?"

90

"Now, before the rush."

And so it began. Most customers phoned first, a few just showed up with their boats. As the weather warmed, boats began to appear outside the shop like lizards coming into the sun. Good weather brought real work instead of painting the shop or chipping the resin off the floor to keep my guys busy.

As May turned to June, the shop hummed with activity. Three employees were no longer enough. I panicked about the amount of work to be done, placed ads in the paper, and phoned Manpower. I hired anybody who said they had experience and put them to work in the shop where I could keep my eye on them.

Summers were crazy. The boating season is short in Vancouver and usually starts in May, running through most of September. Nobody wants to pay moorage for seven or eight months and not use their boat in the summer. Owners wanted their boats working—and they wanted them immediately. To cope, I would hire five or more people to handle the summer crush of work.

I hired Bob in the spring of 1979. He was twenty-five, had red hair, a slim build, and worked for me for a total of twelve years. I didn't know he had a drink and drug problem when I hired him. I grew to like him anyway. He was honest and competent, except for going off the rails a couple of times a year—more towards the end of his employment with me. In the winter, it wasn't so bad if he went missing, but in the summer, it was frustrating. He was one of the best fibreglass guys around and over the years, became competent in woodwork, rail bending, riveted aluminum, transom replacement, and osmosis repairs.

He first disappeared during the second summer he worked for me. We had just finished a large repair to a twenty-eight-foot Carver, which had been stolen and smashed into the dock.

With sea trials completed, we were just waiting for the bow rail to come so the owner could join his friends on their passage to Desolation Sound. Within a few minutes of Eddie bringing the rail into the shop, I dispatched Bob to Mr Hinckley's boat with the rail.

Bob disappeared for three days. He didn't answer the phone or his door. Finally, looking shamefaced and hung-over, Bob walked into my office.

"Where the hell have you been, man? I've been worried sick about you and Hinckley's boat."

"It was partly your fault. The boat was moored by the Raven Pub."

"So?"

"I sat the rail on the deck. A big powerboat went by and caused a wave as I was turning around. I lost my balance and nudged the rail overboard. I didn't want to tell you. I knew we were in a rush. I waited in the Raven for low tide so I could get the rail. But it got dark first. I got too drunk to drive home, so I slept on the boat."

"You slept on the guy's boat?"

"When I woke up next morning it was high tide. I waited on the boat till it was low tide, fished the rail out and installed it. I went to the pub and had a couple beers, getting up the courage to tell you what took so long. When I came out of the pub, the frigging boat was gone."

"Gone? What the fuck do you mean, gone?"

"Just gone. Figured I must have left it unlocked and it got stolen again. I felt pretty shitty about the whole thing and didn't have the guts to tell you. So, I had a few beers and got a cab home."

"Holy shit. I'd better try and get a hold of the owner and tell him his boat's been stolen again."

I finally got Mr Hinckley on the radiotelephone. "Hi, Dave. About your boat ..."

"Yeah, the rail looks great. Thanks for installing it so quickly. A friend of mine lives near the boat. Said he thought a vagrant was living aboard so I went and grabbed it. Didn't want it stolen again. Ha, ha. Just steaming past Hornby Island as we speak. Turns out my friend was wrong. Nothing missing or sign of forced entry—unless the vagrant had a key. Ha, ha. Anyway, the cheque's in the mail and I'll pick up the spare keys in a couple of weeks."

"Good. Glad it worked out, Dave. Have a great trip." I sat back in my chair and my neck muscles relaxed.

About six months after I hired Donna, my part-time bookkeeper, she asked me if I would consider hiring her son Kevin. The family ice business she worked at was closing down and he was out of work. Happy to reciprocate for the good work she was doing for me, I said I would try him out.

He was about twenty, over six feet tall, thin, and never spoke other than saying, "Okay." He didn't seem that excited about work. He knew nothing about boats, so I had him cleaning the shop to start. He was very thorough with cleaning, so I had him clean the boats after we had finished working on them. He could also drive and I had him picking up materials. He was always silent as we sat around the coffee table. I wondered if he had some mental health challenges. After three weeks, I brought him into the office for a chat.

"Do you like working here?"

"It's okay."

"What are your plans in the future?"

"I dunno. Just do the best I can, I guess." With each small job I gave him, he followed instructions and did it well. I tried him on grinding fibreglass, the worst job in the shop—he soon got the hang of it and didn't complain. I showed him how to laminate fibreglass and he did that well too. Gradually, I taught him everything I knew. He learned thoroughly and became the best worker I ever had. He worked for me for the rest of the time I was in business.

Kevin had other talents—he was one of the top motocross racers in BC. I had started racing dirt bikes in hare-and-hound races through the mountains. It was the one time I took my mind off the problems at work.

Riding a motorcycle at high speed over rough terrain required all my focus, and unlike business, I was in complete control and didn't have to rely on anyone. It was me and the bike duking it out alone. I didn't have to talk, explain, apologise, or get upset; I just needed to go as fast as I could. Each blip of the throttle threw me forward; each turn of the bars adjusted my direction. Beautiful and simple—me relying on myself.

Kevin and I started racing together, sometimes at motocross races around the track at Aldergrove, or at hare-and-hound races in the bush. It was a fun thing to do. I taught him some work skills. He taught me some race skills. It was a great way to have fun after work.

ALEXIS STEVE AND MIKE CLEANING THE DIRT BIKES IN THE BACK YARD

Later, I bought my sons motorcycles and we would often go down to the sand flats—before they built the auto-mall—and tear around on our dirt bikes. It was a great way to let off steam and connect by doing "guy stuff" with my sons.

Sometimes, if potential employees phoned for a job, I would ask if they were dirt bikers, thinking maybe we could ride together on the weekends. Because of my accent and the unexpected query, they usually asked me to repeat the question.

◇◇◇

I had been in business about ten years when Billy appeared in my office doorway one July. He was 19, had blond hair down to his shoulders and tattoos covering his short, muscular arms.

"Can I help you?"

"I'm lookin' for work."

"What do you do?"

"Everythin' you do," he said, nodding and smiling.

"How do you know what we do?"

"I worked for Alvis Marine for a year—your competition."

"Okay. You can try out for a week. I'll start you at nine bucks an hour. We work seven-thirty to four. You can start tomorrow."

"Thanks." He turned to leave, then came back. "I walked here from Powell Street. Could you lend me a couple of bucks for the bus?"

I dug in my pocket and handed him a two-dollar bill.

Billy strolled into the shop at nine the next morning.

"You're late. We start at seven-thirty."

Billy smiled and nodded. "What should I work on?" He didn't seem worried about being late. Maybe he had misunderstood.

"Sand the hull of that twenty-four-foot Grew at the back of the shop with 120 grit; we're going to paint it with epoxy, then with Endura." I checked later and he was doing fine.

Billy came in each day at 9.00 a.m. I felt disgruntled that he didn't seem to care that he was late. It was a bad example to the rest of the guys, as if being on time was optional. I decided to fire him when we ran low on work. The start time was the start time.

One morning, I got a phone call from a panicky charter boat owner. One of his customers had fallen through a large window on the side of his boat. He had a fishing charter leaving in twenty-four hours and wanted to know if we could we fix it in time. I said yes. The only guy not on a rush job was Billy.

"Billy, take the truck. Go down to a fifty-three-foot Hatteras at the Royal Van yacht club, dock twenty-three. Take out the broken window and make a pattern of the glass. Take the pattern to Lynmour

95

Glass. It's a rush job. Can you do that?"

Billy smiled. "Yeah. No problem, boss."

Having taken care of that, I set about finding parts for two other rush jobs and Billy slipped out of my mind, until he phoned me three hours later.

"Hi, Rod, how's it going?"

"Why are you phoning? Are you at the glass place?"

"No. I was doing a little personal banking and I ..."

"Personal banking? What the hell do you mean, personal banking? This is a rush job. The guy has fourteen customers going out tomorrow. Get back here as fast as you can with the pattern. Don't talk to anyone. Don't do anything. Just bring that pattern here, right now."

I slammed the phone down and walked onto the shop floor looking for Kevin. He was laying a vinyl floor in a nineteen-foot Hourston Glasscraft. I ranted about Billy doing personal banking in the middle of a rush job. Kevin just shook his head—probably because he was wearing a vapour mask. Half an hour later, the phone rang again.

"Hi, it's Billy. I did what you said, drove back as fast as I could, but I kind of hit the sidewalk. The tire went flat and the rim is bent."

"Where are you?"

"Tatlow and Marine."

"Did you hit anyone?"

"No."

Thank God for small mercies. I slammed the phone down. I told Kevin to go grab the pattern from the truck, deliver it to the glass shop and tell Billy to change the wheel and drive back slowly to the shop. When Billy finally got back, I stared at him as he walked into the shop and gave him the silent treatment. Billy continued with his relaxed 9.00 a.m. start time until a week later, when he arrived at 2.00 p.m. This was too much.

"Where the hell have you been? You're five and a half hours late!"

"I went to that Expo 86 thing in False Creek and seen that Lady Di and Prince Charles. They walked right by me. I was in the front of the crowd. She noticed me and we had eye-to-eye contact. I think she liked me."

I was speechless at this suggestion and about Billy's behaviour in general. In some ways, I admired his chutzpah. He not only lacked a sense of time, but any sense of guilt. In another week, he'd be finished with the job he was on, and I would have to let him go.

I never got the chance. Three days after the Expo incident, he disappeared. No phone call, nothing. He just didn't come in any more—a mystery. Bob said maybe he'd taken off with Lady Di. In some ways it was a relief because it saved me from firing him—always unpleasant.

Four months later, Billy walked into the shop at 9.00 a.m.

"Hi, boss. What am I doing today?"

My mouth fell open. As usual, Billy's attitude was breathtakingly casual. "You aren't doing anything because you don't work here anymore. You left without notice and never came back."

Billy's mouth quivered a bit.

"But I like working here."

"What was I supposed to say to the guy whose boat you were working on? 'Hey, wanna wait around a few months to see if Billy shows up?' The work you did was good, but coming in late every day didn't work for me—then you just took off and didn't even phone to let me know."

Billy looked crestfallen. "Yeah, I was on Vancouver Island. I had some personal business to take care of." He started to leave, then looked back. "Could I borrow a couple of bucks to get home?" I handed the money over, sorry to see him looking so sad. I wondered if Billy had seen some coaching as a kid, or played on a team maybe, whether he would have turned out to be less of a loose strand.

A fortnight after seeing the last of Billy, I met John, the owner of Alvis Marine, in a marine hardware store. "Hey, John, that Billy guy who worked for you, worked for me recently. He came in late every day."

"Yeah, Billy had a problem with that. Speaking of him, did you hear? He committed suicide a couple of weeks ago."

I choked up and left without buying anything. Being an employer was suddenly awful. I went home early and had three whiskies. I racked my brain for what I could have done differently. It was a while before I could tell Louise—two days later, in fact. I felt rotten, like a murderer. I explained the whole thing to Louise. She was shocked, but agreed I couldn't have handled it much differently. It helped me feel better.

Each fall heralded the end of rushing. The phone rang less, the weather cooled and there were fewer of us around the coffee table. It was a relief not to feel pressured every day and have owners upset at me because their boats weren't ready. We sipped our coffee and reflected over the people, accidents and boats the summer had brought us.

As winter approached, we wore warmer clothes as the overhead gas heater struggled to keep the shop at twelve degrees Celsius. Winter was a slim time for work. I tried to keep my core crew employed so I would have their skills for the busy times to come. I also wanted to reward their loyalty.

Such were the patterns of employment in the marine repair business. They followed seasons of the year. For a few weeks in the fall and spring, we had the right amount of people for the work in the shop; otherwise we had too many in the winter and too few in the summer.

Growing the business and hiring staff did not follow a steady upward trajectory. Gains were sometimes followed by losses, ebbing back and forth with the unpredictable tides of business. I grabbed the best employees when I could, held on to them as long as possible, and lost some of them when we ran out of work. What I wanted most was stability. It felt like owning the shop would help provide stability. Why not pay a mortgage instead of rent? Then, if business were bad in the future, not having to pay the rent would reduce stress.

15 - Buying the Shop—Changing Partners

"No man acquires property without acquiring
with it a little arithmetic also."
— Ralph Waldo Emerson

It was 1980, the year the Rubik's cube became popular. I had been in business for four years and succeeded in my goals of feeding the family and paying the house mortgage, but there were still a few puzzles of my own to solve.

My business depended mostly on people having accidents and often felt more like I was rolling dice than operating a business. I always worried about running out of boats to repair. Adding to the type of work we did was one way to increase the workflow, so I bought out my two silent partners and brought in Paul, a new fifty-per cent partner, to work alongside me as the shop mechanic. His buy-in investment paid off the other two silent partners. They were happy. They had made money and we parted friends.

I looked forward to discussing the challenges of business with an in-house partner—someone who could hear and see what was going on in the shop; plus, in his role as mechanic, he would handle all mechanical repairs instead of relying on subcontractors. Every boat engine needed maintenance so we could start to build a regular clientele, rather than just being ambulance-chasers dependent on marine carrion.

Paul had worked for CP Air as an aircraft mechanic but became disenchanted and wanted to try something different. I thought he would be a good fit because he was precise in everything he did. We had been friends for ten years. We were both married with young kids and wanted to do the best we could for our families. I had been badgering him for a couple of years to join me, and finally, he agreed. Paul thought he could learn the marine business quickly, and I believed him.

I, or now we, bought a used Dodge six-cylinder post-office truck and painted big General Boatworks signs on either side. It would serve as a mobile billboard when we worked in marinas. We could also tow boats around, and have a vehicle equipped with parts for our new mechanical department. I built a mechanic's shop above my office and fibreglassed the floor so spilled engine fluids wouldn't leak through the ceiling.

I was pleased with these new operating improvements, but to feel secure, it felt like we needed to own our own shop, so no one could kick us out or arbitrarily raise the rent.

Part of the business buoyancy was due to the booming economy—people had money to spend on boats. However, the price of land rose commensurately, which put buying a shop out of range. I did notice that a building lot close to the shop was selling for $127,000. Buying it would hook us in to the real estate market. We could build later, when we had the money. I talked myself into it, then tried to talk Paul into the idea.

"I'm not interested, Rod. Too much change too fast. I only just started working here. You go ahead though."

I was split down the middle: It seemed like a good idea, but also risky and disappointing that Paul wasn't in.

Louise didn't like the idea either. "They probably won't lend you the money. What if you can't pay it back?"

I made an appointment with the bank. Part of me didn't want the manager to say yes. It was too scary to have another mortgage to pay, but I had to ask, just to see if it was possible.

A man has to have dreams, and mine was to own my own shop. It was an investment in the future. When I retired, I could rent it and we would have a good income. I walked through the door of the TD Bank into Mr Frost's oak-panelled office with my heart thumping, while trying to sound casual.

Mr Frost shook my hand and told me to have a seat. "How can I help you, Rod?"

"Business has been good. I would like to own my own shop. I can't buy one at present but thought getting some land would position me to build later."

I passed him over my financial statements for the past four years, and waited. He flicked through them.

"These look pretty good. You're making twenty percent profit each year; most businesses don't make more than ten. What's your secret?" he asked with a smile.

Fear of failure was the actual answer, but that didn't sound professional. "I do my best to keep costs low and try to please the customers."

"Do you own your house?"

"Yes, but I don't want to risk leveraging that."

"Does your wife own half?"

"Yes."

"Well, don't worry about it. We aren't going to come along with a chainsaw and cut it in half to get the money back from you."

I laughed, nervously. His strange logic had a ring of sense to it. I couldn't imagine Mr Frost out there with a chainsaw on the roof of our house.

"Banks lend money all the time, Rod. It's our business. You entrepreneurs are the creative guys that make the money, which drives the economy. We are just percentage men. We wouldn't be in business if it wasn't for people like you."

Hearing that made me feel pretty good. I had gone there, cap-in-hand, and walked out feeling special about myself and my business—plus, he okayed my borrowing the money to buy the lot.

Shortly after, I signed the multiple papers you have to sign when buying property, which no one reads as the contracts are written in unintelligible legalese. I became responsible for $127,000 of debt and the owner of a vacant lot behind my shop.

I went to look at my new purchase. It was overgrown with dandelions and sat between two warehouses. I kicked some of the dandelions seeds and watched them float through the air. I had done it— grabbed the company a secure base for the future.

Nine months later, I sat at my desk leisurely slitting open my morning mail with a bronze paper knife. I always hoped for cheques, but this time got a surprise. There was a letter telling me not to pay the rent to the landlord, but to a receiver. Mica Holdings must be in financial trouble. Maybe they would sell this building for a good price. I got in my car and drove to the office where I usually delivered the monthly rent cheques to Mike.

"Hi, Mike. I got this letter in the mail telling me to pay the rent to someone else. What's going on?" He looked surly.

"You know, business ups and downs."

"Are you interested in selling the building?"

"We never sell buildings, but in this case, maybe. I will talk to my brothers and get back to you."

His secretary phoned me a week later to come in for a meeting. Mike, his lawyer, brother, and accountant were there.

"You wanna buy the building? We need about $325,000 to cover what we have into it."

I didn't respond immediately. They must be interested in selling but were asking high.

"Sorry, guys. I guess I've wasted your time. I can't afford anywhere near that. I just bought a lot behind your building, so money is tight."

"What could you afford?"

I waited a few minutes. They all looked at me. Finally, I said, "I was thinking more like $240,000."

They looked at each other, then the accountant spoke up.

"What about $255,500?"

"$255,000 could work," I said, trying to sound offhand to conceal my excitement.

The warehouse was six thousand square feet on a double lot. I had just paid a little less than half that for an empty single lot. It would be like getting the warehouse for free. There was a divider wall down the centre of the warehouse. I currently rented half the warehouse; the other half was rented to an auto shop. If I bought the shop, rent from the other side would help pay the mortgage. It seemed like a great deal.

"For that price, we'd need to move fast. Check your financing.

Get back to us within two weeks when it's lined up," said Mike. We shook hands, and I left.

My heart raced as I walked towards my car. I could sell the empty lot and buy the double warehouse. With a building and rent coming in, it was obviously a better investment than a vacant lot full of dandelions. I made another appointment at the bank again, confidently thinking of Mr Frost not cutting my house in half with a chainsaw.

"Sorry, Rod. Can't lend you the whole $255,000. You'd have to come up with about $80,000 of your own money to show us you're serious."

"But you told me nine months ago how much you admired entrepreneurs."

Mr Frost looked irritated. "I like entrepreneurs because they are creative, but the financial landscape has changed since then."

"I see. Any suggestions?"

"Get creative. Maybe find a rich relative?"

Some hope! My dad had been a welder and died when I was eighteen. I inherited his electric razor, which didn't work when I moved to Canada. Mum was still alive, but not at all rich. I thought about who might help as I drove back from the bank. Aunt Marg— Louise had a nice aunt who was well off and lived in Medicine Hat. I brought up the idea with Louise when I got home.

"I don't think we should ask Marg. It's embarrassing. I don't want to ask."

"I know, but it's a great chance to own our own building and the opportunity won't last. She can only say no."

Louise didn't seem so enthusiastic about owning our own shop. She was worried about incurring more debt. I was too, but somehow, after hearing the banker's praise of entrepreneurs, it worried me less. I just told myself this was how business worked. You borrowed money and forged ahead.

As Louise was iffy about the loan, she suggested I phone her aunt myself. Marg sounded a little surprised and asked me to repeat my request. I explained what a good deal it was—a large warehouse on a double lot and how it would be better to pay a mortgage than rent. Marg said she would think about it and get back to me. She'd probably phone her sister, Louise's mother, to check me out. Each day, I waited for the call.

Time dragged. Three weeks later, she phoned.

"I've been thinking about your request and decided to say yes, Rod. It sounds like a good investment for yours and Louise's company. I'll let you wait till you're ready to start paying me back— give you some breathing room."

I was jubilant and thanked her profusely. The building would become ours. In a buoyant mood, I dropped by Mica Holding's office. "Hi, Mike. The cash is more or less lined up."

"We're looking at another buyer."

My heart dropped into my stomach. "So, the deal is off?

"Well, we told you we wanted to move fast, but we never heard from you."

"I think I can get it in a week."

"Well, whoever comes up with the money first gets the building," said Mike, picking up a pile of papers and heading for the door.

I went into panic mode. I didn't want to rush Marg. I dithered a while, then phoned her and told her the situation. It wasn't my fault, after all.

"I'll wire it to your bank in three days," she said.

I thanked her again and rushed off the see the banker. I told him about the money and asked him to get the loan papers drawn up right away. He wanted to wait till the money arrived.

Bloody bankers!

I gave him Marg's phone number and asked him to phone her and confirm the money was on the way. I was rushing in case the other potential buyer, if he existed, got the property before I did. Mr Frost phoned reluctantly, but seemed impressed with what he heard. He got a staff member to work on the loan papers. I got back to the shop and phoned Mike at Mica Holdings to let him know the good news. He sounded terse rather than pleased.

"Lemme speak to your banker to confirm you got the money." I gave him the number and let Mr Frost know that Mike would phone. A couple of hours later, Mike phoned me to come to his office without saying why.

"What for?" I asked.

"We're gonna talk business," he said.

His real estate agent, lawyer, and brother were there. They said there was another offer coming in for $20,000 higher and did I want to meet that? I was mad but didn't show it.

"Guys, I'm here today with the money. Who knows about tomorrow? Maybe your guy shows up, maybe he doesn't. $255,000 is the limit of what I can afford and what we agreed on."

They asked for a few minutes to discuss it. I stepped out of the room and waited in the hallway. Mike popped his head out of the door and summoned me back into the office.

"We decided to go ahead and sell it to you."

"Okay. Good. I'll put the money together." I acted cool, but inside my heart was pounding. I had pulled it off—bought my own building. I signed the usual plethora of unintelligible papers. The money would change hands in a week. As well as our house, Louise and I now owned a vacant lot and a 6,000-square-foot warehouse.

When I arrived back at the shop, I went next door to tell Dave the mechanic the news that I was his new landlord.

"Yeah, buildings are getting affordable," he said. "I just bought a 2,500-square-foot warehouse myself around the corner on Bay Street. I'll be moving out in three months. Take me a while to fix up the other shop."

I was glad it would be three months. It would give me a chance to find a renter. It seemed the value of buildings was dropping. I hoped I had done the right thing.

16 – Real Estate Low Tide

From 1979 to 1981 real estate prices in Vancouver rose 120%
and subsequently declined 51% over 5 years.
http://housing-analysis.blogspot.ca

Just over a year had passed since I bought the shop, and the incoming phone calls—the source of all work—had slowed down. Then one day, the phone stopped ringing altogether. I went to the office of my new renter next door and phoned my business number. Yes, the muffled tones could be heard through the dividing wall. The phone seemed to be the only thing working in the shop.

Around noon, one spring day in 1982, I set out to do an estimate on the repair of a sailboat keel in Lynwood Marina, and felt something different in the air. The zeitgeist of the boating world had shifted—tilted somehow, in a way that was new to me. I didn't get that job, or the next three estimates the company submitted. It was unusual and worrying. Carefully calculated estimates were our major precursor for getting new work. I prided myself on providing prompt, professional, and reasonably priced estimates. Those three key elements had been a winning combination, and got me about sixty per cent of the work I bid on.

At that time, many repairers gave handwritten estimates which took up to a week to prepare, and were often lowballed compared to the actual cost of the job. Tendering a low estimate sometimes worked with individual owners, but not with marine surveyors.

Not getting four jobs in a row worried me. Business should be picking up in the spring, not falling off. Doing what had always worked was suddenly failing. I lowered my prices and started bidding on jobs just to break even—to keep my guys working and pay the bills. I started taking marine surveyors out for lunch to remind them that we still existed. I stopped buying new tools, cut back on Yellow Pages ads, quit supplying free coffee for my guys, and turned the shop heat down a few degrees. To draw in more customers, I made a brochure advertising General Boatworks, had it plasticised, and posted it in every marina in the lower mainland as an inexpensive way to advertise our services.

The cutbacks helped and the brochure did create some business, but the lot I had bought, sold for $5000 less than it cost me and took four years to sell. Real estate seemed to have gone from being a great investment, to a lost cause. Even the big guys were hit hard. 1n 1982, former Vancouver real estate whiz Nelson Skalbania filed bankruptcy for $33 million. His debt was reassuring—my problems were small compared to his.

The whole economy seemed to be on a down cycle. I got a notice in the mail inviting me to attend a debtor's conference for a client who owed me over $10,000 for repairs we had carried out to a thirty-eight-foot pleasure cruiser which had sunk. It was supposed to be covered by his insurance company, Maple Underwriters, but the insurance company had gone broke. I never heard of an insurance company going broke. They had always been a big source of work and secure payment.

I wanted to go and grab all the new equipment we had put on the boat—the batteries, depth sounder, radar, and VHF radio. I phoned the local branch of the Royal Canadian Mounted Police (RCMP) to tell them my plan in case anyone reported us for theft. They suggested getting legal advice. The lawyer I visited gave me some bad news.

"The bank owns that boat. You will be charged with stealing if you do that."

"But we bought all that equipment."

"It doesn't matter. You installed it on the boat and the bank has repossessed the boat."

The lawyer's fee for legal advice was $150.

Other money things were going wrong: I had rented the shop next door to a young guy in the auto repair business. He was about my age, and seemed enthusiastic about having his own shop, just as I had been four years ago. On the fourth month of his three-year lease, his cheque bounced. I walked into his office.

"Your cheque bounced."

"Yeah, it's a new business and it's harder to get customers than I thought. I was wondering if you could give me a month's free rent?"

"Sorry, I'm having trouble myself. You paid the first and last month's rent when you moved in. If you can't come up with the rent, I'm taking the last month's rent for this month and you'll have to move out. I don't have a choice."

They say bad luck comes in threes. It felt like my bad luck was up to number six or seven.

I found a company that wanted to rent the other side of the warehouse—an office furniture manufacturer. A short Romanian guy, about fifty-five, did all the talking. We agreed on the rent, triple net, and the move-in date. Then he introduced me to his partner, Sandy Singh. She had a list of demands—an extra toilet built upstairs, because she didn't want to share with their male workers, a coffee room, new tile in the office, and curtains. I balked. It felt like each thing I agreed to led to another. I got Bernie back in the office with

111

Sandy.

"I'll build the coffee room and toilet, but any other extras you will have to put in yourself. Times are tough." I smiled and shrugged to show them I was friendly but had reached a limit. They signed a four-year lease for $790 a month plus triple net. At least I would have some money coming in to help with the debt load I had racked up.

They turned out to be good tenants, except that Bernie was cheap: he would often come in to borrow a tool.

"I only use once. I don't want to buy. You have, I borrow. Okay?"

I was happy to have reliable renters. I always smiled my best smile and said, "Sure, any time, Bernie."

Personally, I still felt a tradesman's satisfaction about buying a new tool. It meant my business was expanding and I would have the tool next time it was needed.

Harsh economic times did not bode well for the boat business. When people are short of money they tend to spend money on food and housing rather than boating.

My partner, Paul, looked a little grim. He had spent his hard-earned money investing in an industry that was on a downward spiral. Louise didn't discuss business with me, and I didn't want to tell her how tough things were at work, especially after the loan from her Aunt Marg.

The economic downturn produced a few anomalies: Three banks phoned and asked the value of certain boats we were repairing. A typical conversation went as follows: "Hi, this is John Bunce from the Bank of Montreal. You have a Mr Wilson's boat in there, a twenty-eight-foot Catalina sailboat?"

"Yes."

"Could you give me an idea what it's worth?"

"We are not a brokerage. We repair boats."

"I know, but you are in the boating business. Just give me an idea?"

"It's probably in the ball park of five to seven thousand," I said.

"Oh. Are you sure it's not more like $15,000?"

"Yeah, pretty sure. The boat's old and not that well maintained."

I got the feeling that during the days of easy money, banks gave people loans to buy boats based on what they would make on the interest rather than on the value of the boat. With boat values declining, people losing their jobs, and money tight, the value of the asset became more pertinent.

There was also a rash of questionable sinkings. I guessed people hoped their boats would be written off and they could get the insurance money. In one month, three boats that sank came into the shop. On one particular claim, a twenty-six-foot powerboat sank at Thunderbird Marina, the insurance company sent an investigator to visit our shop. He spent a couple of hours combing over the whole boat. Although it was a pleasure cruiser with a galley and dining table, there were no plates or cutlery aboard. The claim was denied.

A bright spot in those tough financial years was the birth of my daughter, Alexis. I loved kids, and to have a daughter after two boys was a huge bonus. I am not a lottery ticket buyer, but that day, the twentieth of May 1983, saw me buy my first lottery ticket ever. Even if the ticket wasn't a winner, I still couldn't lose.

I wondered how to be involved in her life. I had coached both my sons' soccer teams for four years apiece. Would she play soccer, or would she prefer something more feminine? Ballet? It didn't matter—with a daughter, we had children of both genders and my life felt complete.

The only other aspect that brightened those difficult years was coaching soccer. After coaching Steve's team for four years, I coached Mike's team for another four years. I enjoyed the kids a lot, but not always the parents. Many were too intense. I guess after conceiving and nurturing their child prodigies, they expected to see the fruits of their loins kicking butt on the competitive field of life.

"Kick the ball! Kick the ball! Kick the goddamn ball!"

Dads were the worst offenders—the family honour was at stake. I found a fun way to calm things down. We started playing the other teams' parents at half-time. Being *in* the action instead of just watching their fruits play, expended a lot of the nervous energy—being on the field and playing was far more confusing and tiring than directing the game from the sidelines.

Our half-time parent team became quite competent, and when the Seattle exchange team came up, I casually suggested a half-time parent game to our competitive neighbours from the south. They were up for the challenge, but unlike us, had never played together as a team. Some had never played soccer. After our team scored three quick goals, the American goalie picked up the ball, walked slowly up field towards his teammates and said in a loud voice, "My fellow Americans. There is another goal at the other end of this field," and pointed toward the Canadian goal. At least they had a good spirit. We eased up on them and only scored one more goal.

Although business times were tough, Saturday mornings on the soccer field were always a reprieve from the worries of work.

In those challenging financial years, from 1981 to 1986, people's morality changed. Customers who usually paid promptly didn't answer the phone, insurance companies took far longer to pay and some customers asked for financial favours. I remember getting a call from a car dealer.

"Hi, I'm Tom. I've got a car dealership. Had an accident with my twenty-eight-foot Sea Ray. My buddy said you'd do a good job. It's covered by insurance. Can you kinda hide the $300 deductible in the insurance bill?"

"Sorry, I can't do that."

"Why not? I'm a businessman like you. Can't we work something out?"

"I might make three hundred bucks profit on your boat. I would either lose my profit on the repair, or if I added it onto the insurance bill, it might compromise my integrity with the surveyors who are a regular source of work for me. Nothing to work out really, Tom—you understand?" The phone went dead.

I tried to run an honest shop and didn't want the extra worry of illegal or immoral activities. It was tough enough to survive, without compromising future business.

There was one problem caused by the economic downturn that eventfully had a satisfying conclusion. Guido Bruno had a twenty-eight-foot Uniflite which had come into the shop for a minor fire. Mr Bruno would come into the shop, just at quitting time, and start screaming at me. Usually, it was about some minor thing. I couldn't figure out why he was always yelling over nothing. He was an excitable guy, originally from Argentina. Then I found out he was a litigation lawyer for drug gangs—some people even said the Mafia. I figured he was using me to relieve the cut and thrust of courtroom tension. It didn't make it acceptable though. I thought his behaviour rude and childish.

"One of your workers has put black footprints all over my bloody boat deck," yelled Guido.

I asked him to examine his shoe soles. It turned out they were *his* footprints.

"Is this goddamn boat ever going to be finished? It's been here for two goddamn weeks and its fucking boating season."

As the work on his boat wound up, he brought up another problem. "When I'm on the boat with my family, sometimes we run out of power when we're moored overnight. Can that be fixed?"

"Yeah, we could put in another 8D battery and a higher output alternator to make sure it's charged. Should solve the problem. Cost you about five hundred bucks."

"I see. Well if you do the work, and I'm out there with my family and still run out of power, I'm going to come back here and drop the boat on your fucking head," he shouted. His eyes were bulging and there were flecks of spittle on his face.

I wondered if anyone had ever punched him on the nose. "Well, Guido, we usually make about ten percent profit, so for fifty bucks we would make on that installation, it's not worth the risk of getting the boat dropped on my head." I smiled at him, to let him know I wasn't cowed by his yelling.

When we finished the work, Guido paid his deductible and the boat left the shop. Usually the insurance company sent the cheque to us, but I never received the money for Guido's boat. When I phoned to find out why, they informed me they had sent the money directly to the owner at his request. It was obvious why. I could imagine they'd buckled under the yelling. There was no answer to my repeated phone calls to Guido.

Three weeks later, I answered the phone to an unfamiliar and soothing voice.

"Hey, Rod, just wondering how you're doing. How's business?"

"Who is this?"

"It's Guido, with the Uniflite."

"Guido Bruno?" His voice was friendly—unrecognisable from the bombastic screamer I had come to detest.

"Rod, I've been meaning to phone you about the $3,000 I owe for the boat repairs. I'm going through some very tough times. I've lost over a million dollars in real estate in the last month—and I've sold the boat."

"You sold the boat? You haven't paid for it yet."

"Yes. I had to mortgage the house too. I'm even having trouble putting food on the table for my family. I realize you don't want to hear this, but I can only pay twenty cents on the dollar. That's the deal, Rod."

My anger had been rising as I listened to Guido's whiny voice listing all his hardships. It was a cold anger.

"Oh, yeah? Here's the real deal, Guido. Your insurance company paid you for the work we did and now you have to pay us. You're a lawyer and a member of the Law Society, and if you rip people off like you are trying to do to me, I'll report you to them and you'll get disbarred. You can pay me $300 a month until it's all paid off. I will charge you current bank interest on the outstanding amount."

The whiny voice came back, "Rod, you wouldn't do that to me, would you?"

"Miss a payment and find out." I slammed the phone down.

After his usual screaming rudeness, the change to a conciliatory, whining person made me even angrier, because it proved he could be nice. If there was one guy in the world I was not doing any favours for, it was Guido Bruno. I never showed any anger to customers, it was just business, and I tried never to take it personally, but he was the exception. I got the three hundred a month until it was paid off, including interest.

Through a combination of creativity, belt-tightening and tenacity, we pulled through the five lean years until things returned towards normal in 1986. Normal, except for my motorcycle crash and losing Paul.

17 - Unexpected Turns

"A bend in the road is not the end of the road
unless you fail to make the turn."
— Author unknown

The road ahead had more than one bend. A month after each calendar year I met with Ed Ford, our accountant and customer. It was a nice annual ritual where I was used to getting good news about the company's finances. We had made a profit every year. In 1980, we made $41,000. It had been a lot less during the recent lean years, but we'd still managed to make a small annual profit. It was January 1987. With the coming of Expo 86, the economy had picked up.

"How much did we make in 1986, Ed?"

"You made one hundred and fifty-four dollars."

Ed had a sense of humour. "No, what did we make for the whole year?"

"One hundred and fifty-four dollars."

"Is that like for tax purposes or something?

"No, that's what you actually made."

"Holy shit. What was the gross turnover?"

"Four hundred and thirty-eight thousand."

It had been a bad year. My partner, Paul, decided to leave, which forced me to buy him out. Plus, I'd suffered a disabling motorcycle crash. Both events had taken their toll.

I started racing dirt bikes in 1983. The thrill of racing was a distraction from the summer craziness of overwork. Each Tuesday, I drove out to Aldergrove after work and raced motocross. On the weekends, I competed in hare-and-hound races through the mountains. The Sasquatch was the biggest cross-country race in Canada, with over a hundred competitors all starting at once. I'd bought a new bike, a 500 cc Honda CR two-stroke. It was like riding a tiger. Cranking the throttle caused a horrendous exhaust crackle, arm-stretching torque, and you found yourself blasting into what had been the horizon three seconds previously. It was scary and exciting.

Up by the tailings pond in the mountains, past the town of Hope, my Sasquatch race ended abruptly as I careened into a ditch at about fifty miles an hour. Stupid, because I knew the ditch was there, but forgot about it during the excitement of the race.

I broke my right collarbone in four places and damaged my back badly. I could hardly breathe, and lay there for about half an hour in the 40 C heat, spitting sand out of my mouth before anyone found me. They took me down the mountain in a pick-up truck, then by ambulance to a hospital in North Vancouver. I passed out a couple of times on the way. I waited without drinking for three hours to have surgery. They decided not to operate. Racing in the heat is thirsty work. After six hours without water, I was really dehydrated. I complained and they bought me a Dixie cup of water, before loading me into a wheelchair. Louise pushed me to the car. Louise said she had a premonition that something would go wrong when I was racing that day.

My back hurt so much that I could only sleep a few minutes at a time. I tried to run my business from home, taking notes and phone calls with my left hand. My writing is bad with my right hand and pretty much unintelligible with my left, which left me struggling to read my notes after the calls. I could only sit upright for half an hour, then I had to lie flat again.

It was summer and we were very busy. After a week at home, I went back to work with my right arm in a sling. I lay down on the office floor and put the phone close by. When the phone rang, I tucked it under my chin and took brief notes with my left hand. I could lie down fine, but had to be helped into a chair when customers came—it might have disturbed people to do business with someone laying on the floor. At least, while physically present, I could talk to my guys. It was good that Paul was there—someone to help with customers and employees.

We had about six boats that we were working on. One was a big job for a wealthy lawyer, Butch Lewski—a tall, commanding man in his mid-forties. He was putting more sleeping quarters on his boat so his teenage daughter could bring her friends on family boating trips and have no excuse to stay home. He didn't want her staying home alone.

The estimate had been around $3,500, but during my week's absence, Butch got my guys installing a new shower, headliner, propane heater and cabinetry, which cost another $2,000, but he tried to stick to the first price.

"You weren't around, Rod. I was practically doing your job for you, running your crew. You have to allow for the time I spent. My normal rate is $300 an hour."

In the end, I got him to pay for all the new equipment and half of the extra labour costs. My negotiating skills were at a low ebb. Driving to work with my arm in a sling, changing gears with my left hand and trying to run the business lying on my back while gulping down painkillers took its toll.

One customer, who had brought his twenty-four-foot Grew into the shop the Friday before my accident, was a medical doctor. He saw how I walked into the shop, bent over and tilted to one side.

"I don't think I can help you out, Dr Menton. I can't even get on a dolly and roll under the boat to do an estimate."

"I can see you're in bad shape all right, but I want my fucking boat fixed. I've got a holiday planned. I already phoned other repairers and they are all busy."

It showed me where I stood. For some reason, this guy also phoned Louise and told her not to let me race motorcycles any more—maybe so I would not disrupt any future repairs?

Six weeks after I returned to work, Paul informed me that he wanted to leave. It was a big blow. It felt like being discarded. Usually, each of the hard knocks I survived made me stronger, but Paul leaving meant I was losing my friend, my partner, and my mechanic. Paul was close-lipped about why.

"Time to move on, Rod."

Maybe he had learned the job well enough and the economy was picking up, so his future looked brighter on his own—without fibreglass dust floating around the shop.

Having a business partner is much like being married. You hope you have enough common interests to keep rubbing along after the love affair is over. Losing Paul was like a divorce. We figured out what the net accounts receivable were, what the goodwill value of the business was, and he got fifty per cent. We parted coolly, but more-or-less on good terms.

Things were getting tough at home too. My sixteen-year-old son Steve was doing what most spirited teens do, challenging parental authority, by coming home late or staying over with friends. He started attending an alternative school for the academically less inclined. The more we remonstrated with him, the tenser things became. It wasn't pleasant for any of us and Steve coped by leaving home for a while.

We knew he was around, we just didn't know where. We phoned the police, but they guessed he was just a teenager who didn't want to live at home. He might be six-foot-three, but he was still our family— still our son. It felt awful with his bedroom empty night after night, and scary.

Had we been too tough on him?

Now he wasn't here it was more worrying than when he had been here. He was living with one of his friends and returned home a month later. Parenting was trial and error.

Whatever the situation at home, the business ploughed on at its own pace and demanded my full attention. Each winter, I stressed over the lack of work, became happier as things picked up in the spring, got overwhelmed in the summer, and relieved in the fall when the pace slowed down. Each season brought its own challenges.

18 - Repairs by Season
"Summertime is always the best of what might be."
— Charles Bowden

"The Vancouver Coast and Mountains region is home to some of the finest recreational boating playgrounds in the world," claims the bc.gov website.

This upbeat description may well be true in the summer. By contrast, North Vancouver, where my shop was located, receives ninety-seven inches of rain per year—most of which falls between October and May.

Winter brings certain types of damage to a boat: heavy snow followed by rain, can weigh down a canvas top so that it collapses the support bars and breaks the windshield. For boats moored in boathouses, the weight of wet snow sometimes pushed the boathouse roof down so far that it damaged the flying bridge. For boats with cored decks, where there was previous ingress of water, sub-zero temperatures increase the area of delamination as the water freezes and forces the deck apart.

The few hardy souls who went boating in the winter faced heavy rain, decreased visibility and debris, dragged down by engorged mountain streams as they hurtled into the ocean.

Some accidents happened when people weren't even boating. Rob Marchand's case was unusual—not only did it happen when he wasn't boating, his boat suffered the same accident for four consecutive winters.

Rob was in his early fifties, had been super-successful in the Australian mining industry, and lived in a beautiful home on the water. After a busy summer, the seventeen-foot ski boat was left where it was last used, with the bow facing the shore, and tied to Rob's dock in Indian Arm. As winter approached, falling leaves settled into the outboard well. Dampened by rain, they formed a partial membrane across the two one-inch drain holes. The oversized, heavy outboard only gave the transom about six inches of freeboard.

When the Carol Ships Parade of Light passed by on their joyful Christmas journey up the inlet, each large vessel that passed by lapped a few inches of water over the transom, until the boat finally sank at the dock.

Rob would phone us. "Hi Rod, it's Rob Marchand. The ski-boat sank at the dock again. See what you can do?"

"Sure. We'll get it into the shop and do an estimate."

After all the winter sinkings, and possibly encouraged by increased insurance premiums, Mr Marchand took the ski boat out of the water in the fall and put it on a trailer in his driveway for safekeeping. It was not to be. Rob phoned me in late October.

"Rod, my son and his buddy took the boat out for the last ski of the season. After pulling it out of the water on the trailer, they were towing it to your shop to winterize the engine. Somewhere between Cates Park and the Indian Reservation, the trailer came off their car. I guess it wasn't hooked up right. You know kids, Rod. Could you pop along there and see if you find it?"

"Is it on the side of the road?"

"No, they drove back but couldn't see it. They think it must have veered down that ravine into the forest to the left of the road."

"Veered down the ravine?"

"Yeah, somewhere between the res and Cates Park. Have a look, will you?"

Kevin and I took the truck and about 200 feet of rope. We parked and walked along the side of the road, looking for crushed undergrowth. After twenty minutes, we saw a fresh trail of broken salal bushes and ferns between the trees. We followed the trail down. We noticed a tiny cedar house on our left, with a big pair of boots on the front porch. After about forty yards, we saw the boat a further twenty yards down. It was half off the trailer.

We put our backs against the boat on the steep slope, pushed hard, and managed to manoeuvre it back onto the trailer. A presence in the forest made us look up. A Squamish man, about forty-five, with a long pigtail and folded arms, was silently watching our struggles.

"We're getting this boat back on the trailer," I said, feeling as though we were trespassing.

"Yeah," said our observer.

"We'll soon be outta here."

"Yeah." He nodded knowingly, as though boats and trailers often careened off the road into the forest. "I smelled a bear here a little while ago," he said.

"I guess it ran off pretty fast when it saw this boat coming down," I replied.

"No doubt," he said, nodding.

I cranked the winch handle to get the boat snugged up to the trailer mast. When I looked up again, our observer had disappeared. We tied the rope to the front of the trailer and the other end to the towing ball on the truck. When the road was clear, I let out the clutch and drove twenty feet across the road, then waited a few seconds until I heard a distant "Okay," waft up from the forest. Kevin had blocked the trailer wheels and I reversed the truck back across the road. I re-tied the rope to the truck's towing ball eleven times. Each foray *across* the road hauled the boat twenty feet up the ravine but was made in-between vehicles going *along* the road. One final pull popped the boat and trailer out of the forest, bent, battered and covered in foliage, but rescued.

"Wow, that was different. Talk about finding a needle in a haystack," I said to Kevin. I felt elated that we had found the boat and got it out of the ravine. "Do you think there was really a bear there, or was that guy was just trying to scare us off?"

"Hard to tell," said Kevin.

We drove back to the shop, informed Rob we had retrieved his boat, and I typed out a damage repair estimate.

◇◇◇

As a rule, people tend to put off spending money when there is no immediate gratification. Pleasure boat captains were no exception, so damage occurring at the end of the season was often neglected until good weather arrived.

When the sun finally burst through the clouds, warming and lengthening the days, it awakened dormant dreams of boating and lured boaters magnetically towards the water. The more the sun shone, the more the phone rang:

"General Boatworks."

"Hi, can I bring my boat in? I need it fixed right away."

"What's wrong with it?"

"We hit the dock last year and damaged the bow."

"Okay. We're pretty busy, but can probably start on it in a week."

"You don't understand," said the voice, getting much louder, as though I was having hearing problems. "We have relatives coming from Saskatchewan and we're going boating on Saturday. I need it fixed by Friday!"

I didn't like being yelled at but remained calm. "We weren't busy all through the winter, but now there are five boats ahead of you. The soonest we could get to it is in a week's time."

The unhappy boater hung up. A raised voice in primates indicates an attempt to control a situation—in this case, a failed attempt. The whole boating world was trying to get seaborne.

"Gotta get my boat fixed right away," conversations took place from mid-April to June, either by phone or in the parking lot outside my shop. I knew how excited people became when boating season arrived, and their disappointed voices left me feeling inadequate when I couldn't meet their needs.

The start of the season uncovered the invisible damage of winter. "My engine won't turn over," was a sign that the battery had expired or the engine cooling water had frozen and cracked the engine. "My engine oil's turned grey," also meant water in the engine due to freezing damage. Replacing the battery was easy; rebuilding the engine meant a three-week delay in boating and a big expense for the owner.

The call of the open water seemed to jog boaters' memories: "I

126

hit a deadhead in October, but was pulling it out for the season anyway.''

New damage became apparent: "I jumped into my nineteen-foot runabout and went through the floor. Looks like it's rotten."

Fibreglass laminated over wood stops air flow and retains any moisture that has found its way in; the addition of summer warmth creates the perfect conditions for brown rot, which turns wood into the consistency and colour of chocolate.

To repair the decks of runabouts, we replaced the rotten areas. Sometimes, the stringers under the floor were also rotten. Stringers are long pieces of wood running the length of a powerboat hull to stiffen it and provide a landing for the plywood deck. Once the flooring has been removed, rotten stringers can be glassed over with three layers of mat and roving bonded on to the hull; this makes a rigid channel to give the same stiffening effect on the hull as the original wood. Transom wood also rots. This can be dangerous, because the thick plywood helps take the thrust of a stern-drive or outboard motor. If you put your foot on the stern drive or outboard motor and push downward, you can see the transom flexing if the wood is rotten.

The fix is to remove all the plywood and bond two new sheets of three-quarter-inch ply across the inside of the transom to restore its structural strength. It's *not* to replace the rotten parts with plywood patches or pour epoxy resin into the voids, as I have seen suggested in some do-it-yourself magazines.

Along with structural soundness, boat captains often wanted their marine mistresses to look pretty for the season. From the factory, fibreglass boats look shiny and wonderful. After a while, the hull becomes chalky due to oxidation from ultraviolet light. The shine can be restored by applying cut polish with a lamb's-wool hood, tied onto a seven-inch disk sander. The mild abrasive paste takes off the chalky layer of gel coat and adds a wax polish to the hull. As the outer skin of gelcoat is point three to point five millimetres thick, this can be done numerous times.

We often got one or two aluminum car-toppers early in the season with their bows crushed in. Most gas stations with overhangs are high enough to accommodate a camper, but not a camper with an aluminum boat slung on top. Often, the camper owner had been eyeing a neighbour's car-topper through the winter and planning to borrow it so he could not only camp, but fish as well, when the weather finally warmed up. On the way to the lake, with the driver thinking more about fishing than driving, there would be a crunching sound as the camper pulled into the gas station, which nixed the fishing.

"Will it show there was damage when it's fixed?"

"No, you won't be able to tell. I'll order a new bow stem. It'll take a week to get here and five hours to replace the damaged one."

"Okay, just do it as fast as possible."

ALUMINUM BOAT DAMAGED WHILE STOPPING FOR GAS

As the boating season progressed, our work changed from preparations for *going* boating to repairing the results of *having been* boating.

19 - Explosions, Fires, and Sinkings
"A spark neglected makes a mighty fire."
— Robert Herrick

If I were judging the degree of difficulty for boat repairs, I would hold up a ten in each hand for fires. Fires can happen in any season and are sometimes caused by heaters or lamps left on through the winter to keep boats dry, other times by gasoline or propane explosions. The destructive effect of fires sometimes made it difficult to know what the interior had been like prior to being burned. It also had a devastating effect on the owners, who were sometimes too traumatized to tell me or remember what their boat looked like prior to the fire.

Explosions are probably the most dynamic of any boating accidents and are sometimes followed by fire. I got a call one spring morning from a Mr Smythe. He sounded apologetic for bothering me, possibly a little leftover chagrin for having caused an explosion aboard his boat.

"I'll pick you up in my truck and we'll drive to Deep Cove together."

He arrived in a battered Datsun pickup with his Jack Russell dog. As we shook hands, I noticed he had no eyebrows. He had retired recently and decided to install a natural gas stove in his boat. There must have been a leak. As he lit the gas to heat the water for a cup of tea, there was an explosion.

The three of us got out of the truck and walked to the dock at Deep Cove Marina. His dog stopped and sat down at the marina gate.

"Guess he's got more sense than I have," noted Mr Smythe. "Damn dog won't set a paw on the boat since it blew up. Won't even come onto the dock."

We walked onto the boat. The explosion had blown out all the windows and the flash of flame had glazed the surface of the nylon cushion covers. Luckily there was no fire after, and, as he was wearing a hat and gloves due to the cold weather, the owner suffered no injuries except the loss of his eyebrows and his canine boating companion. Few escape an explosion so lightly. He was lucky there was no ensuing fire.

While explosions are bad, fires can do a lot more damage.

I recall sitting with Bill, a forty-five-year-old red-haired schoolteacher, on his forty-four-foot sailboat in Port Moody.

"What was here?" I asked, pointing to a lumpy black mess.

"I–don't know." He sat down and held his head in his hands as his body shook. Tears dripped silently onto his jeans.

The boat had been his after-school project for the last five years. He'd bought the hull and was fitting it out himself. Now he could hardly stand being aboard. The object of hundreds of hours of caring craftsmanship resembled the bottom of a barbecue. The acrid smell of burned headliner, electrical wiring and wood, hung heavy in the air. One of his students was later charged with arson in connection with the fire.

"Why don't you get me the plans you used for building the boat and we'll go from there?" I held his arm as we stepped off the boat back onto the dock. During the three months it took us to finish the boat, I never saw him smile.

Another fire story sticks in my mind, more for the circumstances surrounding it than the damage. We stood looking at the demolished cockpit of Melvin Brown's twenty-six-foot sailboat. He explained that his girlfriend had been reluctant to join him on his sailboat but he had promised to wine and dine her. They had sailed north of Bowen Island and enjoyed a few glasses of wine in the cockpit. He had lit the Hibachi for steaks and suggested they retire to the cabin for some afternoon delight while the steaks cooked.

"She started screaming. I just thought she was enjoying herself, but then realized she was terrified. She started yelling, 'Get me off this boat! Get me off this boat!' I looked back and saw a wall of flames outside the cabin door. I picked her up, carried her towards the cockpit, and threw her through the door-well over the port side. There were fewer flames on that side," he explained. "I threw a life jacket after her, then she started yelling for her purse, so I threw that to her as well. Women are funny, eh?"

Luckily, he had a large fire extinguisher in the cabin and managed to put the fire out. Melvin explained that his lady friend wouldn't get back into the boat, but just clung to the ladder on the transom. Another vessel reported the fire and the coastguard towed them back to the dock.

We rebuilt the whole cockpit for him. He was lucky his propane tank hadn't blown up. I kept thinking about the incident. I wondered what the guys from the coastguard must have thought when fishing his girlfriend out of the water, clad only in a life jacket and clutching a purse. (See the back cover)

Sinkings usually occur either when a boat hits something while under way, or at the dock due to the failure of fittings meant to keep the water out—usually a thru-hull valve. While there is a lot less visible damage than with a fire, the boat's interior usually gets beaten up due to chafing from floating objects, and everything gets coated in a fine layer of oil as it seeps out of the engine.

As boats are looked upon with pride by their masters, I shared many sad moments commiserating with anguished pleasure-boat captains as they lamented over the damaged and dirty countenances of their boats' normally pristine interiors.

As most people were emotional about their vessels getting damaged, letting them vent their concerns was therapeutic and often helped me understand what specific areas were important to them. Usually, that was the case, but it's the exceptions that make life interesting.

Dave Milton was in his late sixties. He wore a cloth cap and a brown corduroy jacket, which smelled of camphor. He had just arrived down from Powell River and we stood silently on the shop floor looking up at his dark-blue, thirty-two-foot Grenfell pleasure cruiser. A few of the clinker-style planks were chafed from the recent sinking. It was December 1987 and Dave's boat had sunk at the dock. His 8D battery had gone flat, so the bilge pump wasn't able to do its job of keeping water out of the slightly leaky wooden boat. The lowered freeboard put the head below water. The gate valve to the head's water intake wasn't closed due to the spindle shaft having corroded off the handle. Water came through the head and submerged the boat.

The boat mover hauled the boat down to our shop from Powell River.

"Can we go aboard, Rod?" said the owner.

"Sure," I said, bracing myself for a long and sad list of concerns. He walked around the deck, then through the sliding back doors into the cabin. I followed him. He surveyed the scene. Everything was coated in oil. Much of the once-glossy mahogany cabinetry was scuffed, oily and needed refurbishing. The headliner was ripped and hung down; the wiring had turned green at the terminals; his charts were all soaked, the upholstery grimy and a side window was smashed. Dave looked from side to side like a turtle taking in the whole scene.

After five minutes of silent staring, he walked towards the fridge, opened the door and took out two Lucky Lager beers. He unscrewed the lid of one and passed it to me. He unscrewed the other and took a swig. I followed his lead. We sipped in silence. I thought the beer might loosen his tongue—it didn't. The beer wasn't cold and there was a slight residue of engine oil on my lips as I drank. It was ten in the morning. Dave kept scanning from side to side as he drank, taking in all the damage. We climbed back down the ladder to the shop floor and looked up at the boat, then at each other, as we drained our beers.

"So, you'll fix her all up like new, Rod?"

I wiped the oil from my lips with the back of my sleeve.

"Yeah, we'll get it back in great shape for you. I'll phone you if I have any questions."

"You gonna rebuild the engines?" They were twin Chrysler hemis.

"Yeah. I have a work order in the office with a list of all the work to be done."

He followed me to the office and signed without checking the list.

"How long?"

"Ten weeks or so."

"Okay, give me a buzz when it's ready."

"Okay. Thanks for coming in, Dave." He shook my hand and left the shop.

I went looking for Kevin. "Hey, Kev, see that guy that just left?"

"The sinker owner?"

"Yeah, we went aboard his boat and he pulled two beers out of the fridge. We drank one each. He never said a word about the damage. Then he signed a $14,000 work order without even looking at what we were going to do, and left."

"Weird. Maybe he was upset," said Kevin.

"Yeah, maybe—hard to tell."

When owners talked more, it helped us understand what had happened, because we weren't there at the time and only became involved after the event. Unfortunately, we were about to experience a one-time change in the usual order of things, and be there when the accident happened.

20 - Collateral Damage
"When ill luck begins, it comes
not in sprinkles, but in showers."
— Mark Twain

I was glad we had finished working on Cameron's thirty-six-foot, wooden Chris-Craft cabin cruiser. Old wooden yachts can be a repairer's and owner's nightmare. The sun, rain, frost, and salt air hack into the vulnerable wood surfaces and make repairs difficult to estimate—there's always a bit of hidden rot. The exterior surfaces need so much maintenance that we often worked on them for close to cost because the owners couldn't afford to pay the full price.

It was March 1987, and we weren't busy. At least the old wooden cabin cruiser had given Jim, a new employee from England, something to work on. Being an immigrant myself, I knew the difficulty of finding work in a new country and had been happy to be his first employer.

Cameron, a tall financial advisor in his late forties, had a penchant for dark suits and wooden boats. We struck up a good relationship when Cameron discovered I had completed my apprenticeship building planked vessels. An enthusiastic first-time boat owner, he wanted to make his new toy perfect. He struggled against my sound advice—that his dream of "getting it back to the wood" was expensive nostalgia from a bygone era of glossy, mahogany cabin sides. Sanding, staining and varnishing the whole superstructure could make it look good, but three seasons exposed to the elements would start to burn through the varnish and destroy the pristine finish.

"Just paint it brown, Cameron. No one will notice the difference from ten feet away."

"I'll notice. I like the look, feel and smell of varnished wood," he said, nodding.

"If you get a hankering for that, just pop inside your cabin and enjoy your nice, varnished mahogany interior. To get the outside of your cabin back to varnished wood will cost you $2,000, compared to $400 for paint. Even then, it may not look great, because we're bound to find lots of rot when we strip off the existing paint." I was making sense—too much sense. He looked sideward at me and mumbled as he signed the work order. We left his boat in the water at the marina as we repaired the wiring, tuned the engine, and painted his white cabin sides a mahogany brown.

A week after we finished, Cameron phoned me and said his bilge pump wasn't working. I sent Jim, the new worker from England, down to the dock where the boat was moored. I returned to paying bills.

An hour later, the phone rang. I recognised Cameron's voice, but couldn't get his meaning.

"I hear you guys blew up my boat."

"What are you talking about? I just sent Jim down to fix your bilge pump."

"The guys from the marina just phoned me and said my fucking boat blew up."

"Your boat—blew up?"

"Yeah."

I dropped the phone. My blood ran cold. My stomach started heaving. I recalled hearing an emergency vehicle siren head towards the marina half an hour previously. I suddenly knew how generals feel when they send soldiers into battle to die.

In a daze, I stumbled out of the office towards my car. What would I find at the marina? *Was Jim dead?* I wanted to know. I didn't want to know. I crawled along in second gear for the three blocks to the dock. My insides felt empty.

I walked down the ramp towards Cameron's boat. A subdued group had gathered a little distance from the smoking hulk. The acrid smell of burnt gasoline still hung in the air. Firemen were on the boat.

What had become of Jim?

"Anyone taken off the boat?" I asked.

"I heard they took someone to hospital."

"Was he okay?"

"Dunno."

The windows of Cameron's boat were blown out. There were shards of glass on the dock and on the adjacent boats. A guy was picking up glass and taking it to the garbage. I was chilly in just a shirt. The foghorn's mournful boom rolled across the water. It started to rain.

I drove back to the office, phoned Lions Gate Hospital, and asked if a male in his mid-thirties with burns had been admitted.

"Are you a family member?"

"No, I'm his boss. I want to know if—if he's still alive. If he's going to live."

"Sorry, sir. We can't give any information unless you are family."

"But it's my fault. I sent him there, to the explosion. Well—before it exploded. I need to know if—"

"Sorry, sir, but we can't give any information unless you're family."

"I'm his employer."

"Sorry, sir. Hospital regulations."

"Yes, yes—you've memorised the rules very well, madam."

I slammed the phone down and walked around the office, spilling a string of cuss words. My skin felt clammy, my stomach tight. I went to the supply cupboard and grabbed a distress flare, walked outside and let it off. The *whoosh* and yellow tail of fire as it reached skywards was satisfying. I let off another while the red parachute of the first still hung in the air. I watched them both fall slowly to earth.

I joined the guys at the lunch table and explained that Jim wasn't eating lunch with us because he'd been involved in an explosion aboard Cameron's boat. They looked grim and shuffled in their seats. Bob lit a cigarette and puffed up clouds of blue smoke.

"Holy fuck. An explosion, eh?" said John.

"Is he like—okay?" asked Kevin.

"I don't know. The hospital wouldn't even tell me if he was there."

"Fuck," said Kevin.

We all faced a similar risk anytime we went aboard a powerboat.

Unlike cars, leaking gasoline in boats doesn't fall onto the ground; the fumes stay in the boat—a potential explosion waiting to happen. Cars don't blow up—boats do.

On my way home from work I cruised by the hospital, finally found parking, and pushed through the hospital door. Under a sign that said *Information*, an older blonde lady sat reading a magazine.

"Hi. My brother got brought in this morning from a work accident. His name is Jim Gough. Which ward is he on?"

"I'll check that information for you, sir." It was just *information* for her. I hopped from foot to foot as she consulted her paperwork—answering several phone calls as she looked.

"Here we are, James Gough. Ward B."

He was alive. Alive!

"Thanks." I left the hospital and walked slowly back to my car, relieved that Jim was alive but beating myself up for being too cowardly to see his face. I told myself it was because I didn't want to lie again about being his brother when I reached the ward.

I phoned his wife the next day to ask how he was doing. She told me they had moved Jim from Lions Gate Hospital to the burn unit at St. Paul's and grafted new skin onto the backs of his hands. More relief. If they operated, he couldn't be doing too badly.

The whole situation was shocking—the first time a man in my employ had come close to losing his life at work. It was also worrying for our reputation: Once this got around the marina, how would my company be regarded? People love to gossip. I could just hear them: "Hey, did you hear about General Boatworks? They blew up a boat. The guy doing the repairs almost died."

The uppermost feeling was guilt. Poor Jim, new in the country, now lay injured in hospital. I needed to stick by my worker—help him however I could.

Three days after the explosion, I got a phone call from Cameron's lawyer. He was suing me. I phoned Cameron to try and reason with him. His voice had changed, become harder. The explosion had blown our previous bonhomie out of the window.

"... of course I'm suing you. My boat was fine until you guys went aboard. I was going on holiday this weekend. If you have anything to say, say it to my lawyer."

North Shore News Photo

Jim's wife didn't drive, so four days after the accident, I drove her through the rush-hour traffic downtown to St. Paul's Hospital. I wanted to talk with Jim to find out what on earth had happened. His face was bandaged but he could still talk, although he lisped a bit. His hands were held in the air by a contraption to lessen the pressure on his skin grafts. He looked frail and vulnerable.

Jim explained he'd gone aboard the boat at the dock, noticed the automatic bilge pump switch wasn't working, and flicked on a manual switch located on the dashboard. He looked over the side of the boat to see if it was pumping. To his horror, he saw that the inch-and-a-quarter stream of fluid gushing into the ocean was pure gasoline. He tried flicking off the manual switch but it didn't work; the float switch must have taken over.

When living on a houseboat in England, Jim had experienced a fuel spill which had ignited and set the whole surface of the river on fire. Houseboats were damaged and some people had sustained burn injuries. To avoid a similar disaster, he raced to the aft end of the boat and yanked off the battery cables to stop the bilge pump working. This caused a spark, which ignited the gasoline fumes. The explosion started between his two hands. Luckily, he was wearing a woollen hat, glasses, and had a moustache, which lessened the damage to his face, but the backs of his hands were badly burned.

He had been thrown backwards by the blast and knocked semi-conscious. An off-duty fireman happened to be walking down the dock, saw the explosion, and pulled him out of the boat just as flames were starting to lick up the varnished wood.

"Sorry, Rod. I shouldn't have pulled the battery cables off, but I panicked when I saw the gasoline pumping into the marina." Tears streamed down his face and his chest convulsed. I squeezed his shoulder. His wife, Marci, looked on silently.

We later found that the corroded fuel tank had sprung a leak and dribbled gasoline into the bilge. I let Cameron know my worker had been injured because his gas tank was corroded and that he would be hearing from Jim's lawyer. This wasn't true. Jim wasn't the suing type. I thought it might persuade the owner to discontinue his lawsuit against me. It didn't.

I took Jim's wife to hospital again. She was very appreciative. When I asked her how Jim was doing, she replied that she didn't know because the doctor had always gone by the time she arrived.

"Why don't you ask the nurses to ask the doctor, then they could tell you about his progress?"

"Oh, what a good idea," she said, smiling.

I phoned Jim's wife every few days to check how he was doing. Three weeks after the accident, there was no reply. I tried phoning Jim at the hospital with no luck. I wanted to keep in touch. It had been me that had sent him aboard a floating bomb, that had caused this dramatic downward turn to his life.

I went around to Jim's walk-up apartment and knocked on the door. After a long wait, the door opened.

"Jim, how you doing?"

"Been better, Rod." The kitchen table was full of empty beer bottles and Styrofoam food cartons. Jim showed me the pressure bandages on his hands and explained they were to prevent scar tissue from forming.

"Another thing—I can't bend my elbows." They had become seized because his arms had been held in the air for many days after the skin grafts. I was astonished.

"Jim, you have to sue those bastards. That's crazy! They're doctors. They're s'posed to know what they're doing."

"No. I don't want any bother, Rod. I just want to get better." I couldn't persuade him. He was going to therapy twice a week to try and un-seize his elbow joints.

Jim had other problems: Two days prior to my visit, he had arrived home from the hospital to an empty apartment. His wife had left a note on the kitchen table saying she had left him and taken the $17,000 in their bank account—Jim's redundancy payment from the Royal Navy. She mentioned that she had donated $2,500 to a Christian charity in South America and had moved in with a lesbian friend of hers.

"Jesus Christ, Jim. I can't believe all of this."

"I know—I've got no money. I can't pay the rent or buy food. Marci took everything —even the bloody TV."

Standing there in a dirty T-shirt, rumpled brown cords, uncombed hair, and three weeks' stubble, he was a forlorn figure—an explosion survivor who returned home to a marriage break-up and a pillaged bank account.

"Jim, come back to work. I'll pay you your regular wage. Just do what you can. No pressure."

"I can't pull wrenches like I used to. My elbows barely bend."

"No worries. Just do what you can, mate. We'll figure it out."

I told Louise about Jim's bad luck. She couldn't believe the awful chain of events he had been through and baked a lasagne for me to take to him.

Three days after Jim returned to work, he removed a carburettor from an engine; it made him vomit. He came into the office looking pale and shaken.

"It's not gonna work, Rod. I just got a whiff of gasoline and threw up on an engine."

As Jim couldn't return to his former occupation, Worker's Compensation agreed to retrain him in a new field. I was happy for him, and relieved to no longer be his employer.

Eight months later, I phoned to see how he was doing. He had retrained as a locksmith, but had been unable to find work. He explained he'd had a business opportunity, but the bank had been unwilling to lend him the money to buy a van.

"How much money do you need for the van?"

"Three thousand."

"And the business operation seems pretty secure?"

"Yeah, I've got a partner who is putting in $3,000."

"I'll lend you the money as long as you put the van in my name and pay me back within a year."

"Thanks Rod. I can do that. I really appreciate your help."

Next time I phoned, three months later, Jim told me the van had disappeared. He hadn't wanted to tell me. His partner claimed he had been in an auto accident, which had totalled the vehicle. I decided to stop phoning Jim. My help wasn't working out.

Four months later, I got a cheque in the mail for $3,000. Jim phoned me shortly after. He'd split up with his business partner. Six weeks after that, he'd seen the van parked on Kingsway Street, intact, and full of expensive electrical equipment. He used his locksmith's training to pick the door lock and bypass the ignition, then hopped in and drove it away. He sold the van and all the equipment in it for $5,000. Having been told the van was a write-off, he didn't think his ex-partner had grounds to come after him.

A year after the explosion, Jim met a woman with a lovely house in Delta and moved in with her. She was a retired prison guard who had taken early retirement due a disability; she had three dogs. Jim loved dogs. Finally, some good luck had come his way.

I wanted Jim's accident to have some meaning, so I implemented improved safety protocols for my guys when working aboard gasoline-powered vessels. I also increased my liability insurance coverage—no longer a hypothetical calculation.

After examining all the facts, Cameron's insurance company dropped the claim against me. I was already churned up inside and not having to relive it again in court was a huge relief. The ponderous procedures of the law courts left me cold.

21 - Mary Cummins V General Boatworks

"No man suffers injustice without learning,
vaguely but surely, what justice is."
— Isaac Rosenfeld

The year was 1988—a contentious year: Solidarity's widespread strikes in Poland began to unravel communism. Ben Johnson became the first man to run a hundred yards in under ten seconds at the Seoul Olympics, but was disqualified for using anabolic steroids. Oliver North was indicted in the Iran-Contra scandal for selling American arms to Iran.

To avoid contention in my business life, I had learned to supply customers with a typed work order listing the cost of materials and labour. If anything changed during repairs, such as finding hidden damage, I promptly phoned with updates. It became a point of honour for me to complete repairs on time and on budget. The longer I ran the business, the more I realized that maintaining good relationships with clients depended upon excellent and timely communication.

Despite my insights and procedures, occasional conflicts still arose. If a disagreement remained unresolved, the Small Claims Court was one option. In my twenty years in business, I went to court six times—twice as an expert witness, twice chasing customers for money, and twice being chased for money. I detested going to court. After a few years in business, I decided that if a customer owed me less than $2,500, it wasn't worth the hassle, time, and trauma of going to court. I based this calculation on self-preservation rather than financial considerations.

I feared the courtroom: It seemed to be an alien world of words and insinuation where facts and realities were debatable, even negotiable. My shop life was concrete—a world of results. If you repaired a damaged hull right, it didn't leak; if you repaired it wrong, the boat sank—nothing to argue about.

Dressing up in a jacket and tie, stepping through the courthouse doors and fiddling with sheaves of paper switched my brain off. I had trouble putting words together, making a judge understand the chain

147

of events which had led to the problem. I'd stress over the right things to say before the trial, then go brain dead during the trial. Outside the courtroom, after it was over, I'd say the words that should have come from my mouth—as if that would help. It didn't. You only got one shot, and then the judge ruled. To make judges understand, you had to keep stating the obvious—not one of my strengths. I tend to think and speak in shorthand.

The end of summer signals a nostalgic end to days spent on the water for most boaters. For this reason, Mary Cummins and her friend decided to drive down to her boat in Blaine and grab the last of the late September sun. She loved being on the water in her twenty-seven-foot sailboat. The day was unusually warm and sunny as the twosome set out for a leisurely cruise. They ate a picnic lunch, sipped chardonnay, and admired the shifting landscapes as Boundary Bay drifted slowly by.

When Mary opened the hatch to use the head, black smoke billowed into her face. She shrieked, thinking the boat was on fire and considered jumping overboard, but the life jackets were in the cabin. Peering through the smoke, she could see no flames. That was because her engine exhaust manifold—the system using saltwater to cool the engine—had become corroded and was pumping smoke into the cabin. For some reason, she had left the engine cover off and hot saltwater had sprayed out of the manifold over the boat's teak cabinetry. Luckily, there had still been enough water to cool the engine. They motored the short distance to the dock, turned the engine off and watched the smoke dissipate from the blackened interior. Crestfallen that her beloved boat was damaged, Mary drove back across the border in a dark mood and phoned her insurance company about the incident.

Jim was the marine surveyor hired by the insurance company to ensure her boat repair claims were carried out professionally and on budget. He dropped by my office on his way home.

"Got a little job for you to estimate, Rod. It's in Blaine Harbour, just across the border."

"I'm not crazy about doing an estimate down there, Jim. By the time I've passed through immigration twice, it could take more than three hours."

"We'll pay you for your time—four hours."

"Okay, that's different. What's the job?"

"It's mostly clean-up. The owner, a woman, ran her boat engine for three or four hours with the manifold pumping smoke into the cabin. Some hot saltwater sprayed onto the woodwork."

"She never noticed anything was wrong?"

"Guess not," he said, before chuckling.

I had recently found a solution to something which had been a longstanding problem—cleaning the boats after we'd repaired them. We could do the technical work fine, but were sloppy on the clean up afterward. To remedy this, I found Hanna, a wiry forty-four-year-old German woman who did contract cleaning. After using Hanna, customers had remarked how nice their boats looked inside after a repair. As this seemed like a big cleaning job, I suggested to Hanna that we drive down together. She would be company on an otherwise boring trip south of the border, and could provide a professional opinion on cost. I offered to pay for her time. She was a single mum and needed the money.

We located the boat in Blaine Marina and went aboard. The whole interior was sooty, black, and stank of diesel smoke. Hanna had brought a selection of cleaning agents and got to work on the boat interior, finding what worked. With a lot of effort, the grime came off. She figured it would take eighteen hours to clean the whole inside. Apart from cleaning the interior surfaces, we would have to eliminate the smoke smell from the parts we couldn't reach, refinish some woodwork, replace the headliner, upholstery cushions, sleeping bags, and charts, etc.

I completed the estimate and faxed it off. If the estimate seemed reasonable, I was sure we would get the job as we were the only company bidding.

Jim phoned back. "Eighteen hours to clean the inside?"

"Hey, I took a professional cleaner down to check it out. The stuff is really caked on. If it's less, I'll charge less." This was a concession. If it was more, I wouldn't charge more. I liked Jim and wanted to keep in his good books.

"Okay, that sounds fair. Get the marina to haul it out and a boat mover to bring it up. Obviously, the insurance won't pay to repair the manifold. It's wear and tear—a maintenance issue."

"Right. Thanks, Jim. We'll get on it. Give me the owner's number and I will get her okay to proceed."

I tried phoning Mary but couldn't get through till about 3.00 p.m. She sounded confused. "Why are you phoning me?"

"The surveyor asked me to do an estimate on your boat."

"Do I know you?"

"No. We have never met."

"I didn't ask you to go to my boat. Why were you there?"

"As I mentioned, the marine surveyor hired by your insurance company asked me to estimate the cost of repairing your boat from the recent accident you had."

"What Accident?"

"The smoke damage to your boat."

"Oh, that. Em, yeah, I don't need you. I am going to fix it myself."

"Okay. Are you going to fix the engine too?"

"Em … I dunno. I don't want to discuss this right now."

"Okay. Let me know if you need help."

I gave her my phone number and hung up. I let Jim know that she didn't need our services. It looked like a lost cause. At least I would get paid for the estimate. I turned back to the work at hand.

Two weeks later, I got a phone call.

"It looks like I gotta use you guys."

"Who is this?" The voice sounded vaguely familiar.

"Mary, with the boat." Having a boat was probably an identifier among Mary's friends, but for us, everyone who phoned had a boat.

"Which boat do you have, Mary?"

"The one the insurance won't let me repair. They said I have to use you."

"If this is the sailboat in Blaine Marina, you can use anybody you wish, as long as the surveyor approves. If you want us to repair your boat, you will have to come in and sign a work order."

"I'm not signing anything."

"We need you to sign as proof you agree with us repairing your boat." If we got the job, I hoped the work would be easier than the conversations with Mary.

Mary dropped in a few days later. She was slightly built, had short grey hair and wore an old brown leather jacket. My wife Louise was there, dropping off some papers from the accountant. They met briefly as Mary perused the paperwork.

"What's this—$780 to repair the engine?"

"That's the cost of replacing the manifold; the thing that caused the problem in the first place. Plus a few other items—the fuel filter has water in it, the alternator belt is worn, and your engine oil needs changing."

"Who pays for that?"

"You do—the insurance doesn't pay for wear and tear. It's a maintenance issue."

"With the $300 deductible, it's over a thousand bucks. I don't have that kind of money."

"Well, we don't have to repair the engine."

"The boat's no bloody good without the engine," she yelled.

Louise looked up to see what the commotion was about.

"I can't pay till I get my next cheque. It'll be six weeks from now."

"That should work out. It will take a couple of weeks to repair, and you have a month to pay."

Mary bent over the desk to sign the work order. Louise, on the other side of the desk, raised her eyebrows at me. She was getting an understanding of why I sometimes complained about customers.

The repairs went smoothly. Hanna managed to get the whole

interior looking sparkling clean. She took sixteen hours, which pleased the surveyor. With the new upholstery, headliner, and refurbished teak, the boat looked great. I felt good about the result and phoned Mary. She came by a couple of days later, avoided eye contact, and looked silently around the boat. She reiterated that the insurance company should pay for *all* the work. I repeated that they would not pay for normal wear and tear, such as a corroded manifold.

"Do you want the boat to go back to Boundary Bay?" I asked.

"No, Mosquito Creek. I'm going to live aboard."

"So, I need a cheque for your deductible, Mary. The insurance company will pay me the balance."

"Why do I have to pay a $300 deductible?"

"It's written in your policy that you pay the first $300 of the claim. You could pay a higher premium and pay a smaller deductible."

She got foul-mouthed about the insurance company, signed a cheque for $300 and tossed it on to my desk.

"Thanks. The balance for the insurance work and engine repair is due in thirty days."

I didn't feel good giving her credit, but as she planned to live on the boat it would only cause more fireworks if I didn't release it. "You just need to sign here, Mary, agreeing that the boat has been repaired to your satisfaction and that you'll pay within thirty days." She scowled, signed and stormed out of the office.

I registered a mechanic's lien on Mary's boat. I had never seized a boat, but when payment was not forthcoming, the threat of losing their boat usually encouraged owners to pay. I received the balance owing from the insurance company, but nothing from Mary for the engine work.

As she lived on the boat and didn't have a phone, I made two trips to drop off notes asking for payment, pinning them to her cabin door. On the second visit to her boat, I heard music coming from inside the cabin. I knocked louder, but to no avail.

Busy with my real work of repairing boats, I had let collecting the money for Mary's repair slide, but that was over. It was approaching Christmas and things were slow. It was almost three months since we had completed her engine repairs. Back at the office, I looked at her file in the unpaid drawer and remembered her attitude—resentful, blaming, and ungrateful.

For the first time ever, I called the bailiff and instructed them to proceed with the seizure of Mary's boat. If she paid the outstanding balance, she could retain the boat. I generally tried not to make overdue money a personal issue, but in this case, proceeding with the lien gave me a certain amount of satisfaction.

I presumed they had seized and sold Mary's boat, because two months later, I received a cheque in the mail from the Bailiffs for the outstanding balance. On the very same day, a process server walked into my shop and handed me a summons to attend small claims court: Mary was suing me for $10,000, the maximum allowed.

Written under the "Defective Goods and Services" section was a description of the bad service she had received. She claimed I had repaired the engine without her permission, charged too much, and illegally seized her boat. The $10,000 was for living expenses and emotional damage caused by the seizure.

I felt uneasy. Even though I thought the claim laughable, seeing the charges described in black and white was a shock, worrying—as if it were the actual truth. I rummaged through my files and pulled out Mary's paperwork. Yes, there it was—a signed work order, also her signature on the actual invoice confirming we had completed the repairs. I felt relief. Ten thousand dollars including emotional damages? What a joke. She should experience the emotional damage at my end when people took their boats and refused to pay. Although business went on as usual, the impending court date hung over my head as I sat at my office desk—day-by-day creeping closer. I hated court cases. They were battles of words. I preferred battles with things I could fix.

When the trial day arrived, Louise came with me. It felt good to have support. As Louise had been present when Mary had signed the work order, she might be a useful witness.

We arrived twenty minutes early to find the right courtroom. There it was, posted on the door of courtroom number three: *Mary Cummins versus General Boatworks Ltd., March 19, 2.30 p.m.* It was about to begin. My stomach was fluttering.

They were running late; at 2.45 p.m. the sheriff opened the door. People filed out from the previous case, but some stayed.

Why are they staying? Must strangers watch this sordid struggle?

Louise and I went in and sat down at the front. It was quiet, serious; no one spoke. There was a faint odour of Pine-Sol cleaner. The austere oak-wood seating reminded me of the pews in a church. Judgment day had arrived.

Mary came in behind us and sat to our left. She was wearing a green woollen hat, her old brown jacket and jeans. Her complexion looked sallow. She sat with a smartly dressed woman wearing a black pantsuit, coiffured dark hair and mauve lipstick.

Shit, she's brought a lawyer.

The bailiff, a short guy with a moustache and a brown uniform, stood up abruptly and announced, "All rise for Judge Wagstaff."

We stood.

How did he know the judge was coming?

The judge entered the courtroom. He was a serious-looking man in his fifties, dressed in a red robe. He motioned us to sit down. The bailiff told us to state our names for the record. In a frail voice, Mary gave her name and informed the judge that as she was not feeling well, she hoped her friend, Cecilia Baines, would be allowed to speak for her. The judge agreed and asked Cecilia to proceed to state Mary's case.

Good, she's just a friend.

"This is a simple case of deception and fraud followed by malicious and punitive action on the part of General Boatworks Ltd., which had disastrous, life-threatening consequences for my friend, Your Honour."

What the hell is she talking about? I glared sideways towards

154

Cecilia.

Cecilia continued in a righteous voice, "My friend Mary is a simple woman, Your Honour. She does challenging work in the downtown east side, helping homeless people find their way back into society."

I didn't know that.

"Her way to relax from this challenging work is to spend time on her sailing boat." The judge nodded. "After a particularly hard week, in which one of her clients committed suicide by throwing himself in front of a trolleybus, Mary spent the whole day on her boat with a friend recovering and getting her peace of mind back."

Mary nodded. The judge nodded.

Yeah, that makes sense. Might explain why she didn't see the smoke.

"Something happened with the engine. There was a lot of smoke. Mary wasn't sure why, so to be safe, she motored back to the dock."

"So, the engine was still running?" asked the judge.

"Yes, Your Honour. That's how she got back to her berth. She phoned her insurance company and they sent this man, standing to my right, down to her boat. We think he must be a friend of the insurance company."

What? Like it was some kind of insider deal?

"How so?" enquired the judge.

"They asked General Boatworks for an estimate, instead of putting it out to tender."

She's twisting things. It was in the US. Jim got my estimate and saw it was fair.

"So, General Boatworks got the job and repaired the boat?"

"Yes, Your Honour; that's when the problems started. My friend wanted to live on the boat, but what amounted to a bit of cleaning took almost three weeks, forcing Mary to move into a motel. I have a copy of the bills here."

Bit of cleaning? Motel bills? What a joke!

"Bailiff, can you collect those?" instructed the judge.

155

The bailiff briskly collected the paperwork, his leather shoes echoed on the parquet floor. He passed the bills to the judge, who perused them, made some notes, and passed them back to the bailiff who delivered them to the court recorder.

"Mark these as exhibit one," said the judge, nodding.

This is bullshit.

Cecilia continued. "General Boatworks made unauthorised repairs to Mary's engine and charged an exorbitant amount. They replaced the engine manifold when it could have been patched until Mary had enough money to repair it properly. My friend was not informed of this option. I have a description of a product which could have been used." She handed over the manufacturer's description of the plastic steel repair product to be recorded as evidence.

No way that stuff would have worked. But it's her word against mine

"Then, your honour, the real crime took place." She paused. My friend came home one day, carrying bags of groceries down the dock, and found her boat—her home—had been seized by General Boatworks. She sat on the dock in the rain and wept, Your Honour."

I could picture it. My cheeks burned red.

"Mary is a recovering alcoholic. The loss of her home pushed her into relapse. She started drinking again."

I noticed spectators in the court staring at me. Louise was looking at me. Jesus!

"Because Mary worked with homeless people, she was fired for drinking. You can't help people with drug problems if your own addiction returns."

I am a bad person.

"Mary is a cancer survivor, Your Honour. Sadly, the stress of losing her home, her job, and the return of her addiction took a terrible toll on her health and well-being. Last week she found out the cancer had returned."

Holy shit. I had sent someone to death's door for $780.

"And what is your account of what took place. Mr Baker?" asked the judge.

I had no 'account.' I was stunned into silence by the results of my actions

"Mr Baker, do you have anything to say?"

Mary had cancer? That's why she is wearing a hat and looks sallow.

"Is there is a signed work order, Mr Baker?" The judge asked, tilting his head towards me and raising his voice, "If so, I suggest you submit it into evidence *now*."

I exhaled and opened my folder. The work order was supposed to be on top. I rummaged through the papers. The judge was becoming impatient. My heart raced. I bit my lip and kept searching. I found it, passed it to the sheriff, and the judge perused it.

"This a work order for engine repairs in the amount of $781.47 with the customer's signature agreeing to pay the cost of repairs within thirty days and acknowledging that a repairer's lien would be placed on your vessel. Bailiff, pass this to Ms Cummins."

Mary glanced briefly towards the document, as though it was an annoying insect.

"It's fake."

"Is that your signature?"

"I didn't sign it."

No one spoke. Silence enveloped the room. The judge looked at me, then at Mary, swallowed, and looked down at his notes.

"Yes, you did. I saw you sign it when I was in the office." All eyes in the court turned toward Louise.

"You were complaining that the insurance should pay for everything." Her soft, sure voice rang like a clear bell in the silence.

Her support gave me the courage to speak.

"Your Honour, if I could explain for a moment?" The judge nodded. "The plastic filler she is talking about wouldn't have worked to patch her manifold. It was too corroded, that's why we replaced it. She authorised us to replace her engine manifold; it's on the work order. She said a boat with no engine was no good and that she would pay me within thirty days."

I explained to the judge that I had waited almost three months before I exercised the lien and had posted two notes on her door, telling her the boat would be seized unless payment was received.

"When she didn't pay, she left me no choice. It's the first time I have ever done this—seized a boat. I didn't know all this other stuff would happen to her. I just wanted to get paid for the work we'd done, that's all." I was spewing words, relieving the pressure.

Cecilia jumped out of her seat. "You're making this up. Mary ..."

"Sit down, madam. You will have a chance for rebuttal when Mr Baker has finished."

"I have finished, Your Honour. Except, I've found the invoice Mary signed after examining the boat, agreeing that we had completed the work satisfactorily and that she would pay the balance owed."

The bailiff passed the document to the judge, who read it, took a long look at Mary and Cecilia, and instructed the bailiff to deliver it to Mary.

"Ms Cummins. Is this signature also faked?"

Cecilia jumped up to speak.

"Sit down, Ms Baines. I would like Ms Cummins to answer."

Mary didn't answer. She shifted on her feet and looked uncomfortable.

"Ms Cummins, you are required to answer my question, otherwise I can hold you in contempt of court."

Cecilia jumped up again.

"Miss Baines, that applies to anyone not following my instructions." The judge's voice was getting icy. Cecilia sat down.

"Well, Ms Cummins? And let me remind you, you are under oath in this courtroom." Looking at Mary, the judge waited.

"I can't remember. It's a long time ago. Maybe it's my signature," she whispered.

"Examine the document and tell me whether or not it *is* your signature."

Mary seemed to get smaller in stature. She stared at the paper.

Her lips quivered. I almost felt a tinge of sympathy.

"Yes, it's my signature," she said, in a barely audible voice.

"Ms Baines, do you wish to ask Mr Baker any questions?"

Cecilia stood up slowly; her brisk manner had melted. "I— no, Your Honour. No questions."

"Do you have any questions, Mr Baker?"

I didn't, I just felt relieved.

The judge neatly summed up what had transpired in the case. "While I sympathise with the poor health of Ms Cummins and the loss of her boat, which was also her home, this court is guided by contract law. In this case, Mr Baker was using the legal means at his disposal to recover the money owed him from the repair contract. I therefore deny Ms Cummins her claim for $10,000 in its entirety. Case dismissed."

I had won, but didn't feel victorious. My actions had contributed to Mary's demise. I was healthy and she had cancer. She looked sick and might be homeless. I lived in a comfortable house. I was relieved at not having to pay the $10,000, but also experienced a heavy sadness. I hated courtrooms even more.

22 - Learning from Mistakes with Boats and People

"The only true wisdom is knowing you know nothing."
— Socrates

Another Monday morning, and the persistent ringing of the phone had me scrambling out of a boat, running along the cement shop floor and into the office. The phone, the phone—a bubbling life-spring source of all work. It rang, and I ran. Someone needed something, I responded. I always responded. I needed the work, even if I didn't.

"General Boatworks."

"Em, my name's Cyril. Our boat blew up on the weekend—not sure what to do next. Any ideas?" The voice was mournful.

"Wow, sorry to hear that. What happened?"

"I and my brother-in-law thought we'd try boating and bought a twenty-four-foot Reinell. We launched it at Lions Bay. We were aboard with our wives. The engine wouldn't start, then there was an explosion and the boat caught fire."

"My goodness, that sounds awful, especially for your first time boating."

"Yeah, it was frightening. Then the goddamned marina guy pushed us away from the dock with a pike pole in case we caught the other boats on fire."

"Wow, sounds scary."

"You're damned right it was. We had to jump into the water and swim to the launching ramp."

I imagined this happening—must have been terrifying.

"Anyone hurt?"

"No, just badly shook up. Our wives were screaming."

"I bet. Anyone would be freaked by that kind of experience. Are you insured?"

"Yes, we're insured. What should we do now? I don't want it at Lions Bay any more. I'm unhappy with those guys."

"I could get it brought to our shop for an estimate."

"Sure. Do that, please."

When boaters phoned, they were often stressed. I listened to their concerns. When they'd recovered enough to think, I suggested solutions to their problems—if they were solvable. Even if they weren't, they remembered a friendly voice on the phone for next time.

In their enthusiasm to go boating, the Reinell owners had gone aboard a day earlier than planned, before the mechanic had reinstalled the carburettor. When they tried to start the engine, the fuel pump spat gasoline into thin air and the sparks from the starter motor blew the boat up. Someone had saved money by installing an automotive starter, instead of a marine one equipped with a spark shield to prevent explosions.

Bob, the boat mover, brought their boat to my shop and parked it outside. The damage was severe; half the side was burned away. I stared at the boat and imagined what had taken place. The damage was far beyond the insured value. I offered the insurance company $200 for salvage value and they accepted. Although wrecked beyond use, the burnt-out boat held a couple of unexpected benefits.

One of my workers was careless in repositioning the blocks under a thirty-two-foot Uniflite powerboat; it partially toppled over and fell against the damaged Reinell sitting beside it. The burned hulk prevented the Uniflite from falling right over and causing major damage.

I put an ad in the *Buy and Sell* newspaper and sold the Mercruiser engine and stern drive in the Reinell for $600. I sent the owner a cheque for $200 and told him to take the explosion survivors out for dinner.

I believe the only reason the boat ended up at my shop was because I had learned to listen, sound understanding, and helpful. Empathy goes a long way when you are upset.

Hearing boat owners' stories, their joys, sorrows, and challenges made me realize I was in the people business, not the boat business. It was people that brought the boats in to my shop, and people that paid me, or Okayed their insurance companies to pay me. If I wanted to be successful, I had to please boat owners—not myself, my staff, or the insurance companies.

162

Sounding interested and helpful was the first step for attracting customers but more challenging than providing empathy was providing good results. Good results often rested upon the shoulders of learning from bad results. The indigestion caused by swallowing mistakes was a great teacher. The opportunities for screwing up were many, and fell into two main categories—repair mistakes, and people mistakes.

Boat repairs can go awry from simple errors; owners always phone after to help with the learning.

One scary lesson was learnt about not mixing up boat parts: We were repairing a Hell's Angel's twenty-eight-foot powerboat. In a rush, Paul grabbed and installed the wrong rotation propeller from another customer's boat. When the biker launched the boat at Reed Point and put it in gear, the boat went backward instead of forward. The biker phoned to let us know he was going to "pull the mechanic's face off" if we didn't get down there and fix it immediately. We did.

Forgetting to put the locking pin behind an outboard propeller meant that Mr Halstaff's seventeen-foot Boston Whaler went forward fine, but when put in reverse to stop, the propeller spun off and the boat crashed into the dock. Charlie, one of my mechanics, did this with two different boats. Once was forgivable, twice was embarrassing and I had to let him go. I couldn't risk a third time—someone could get hurt.

Painting the wrong boat happened because I didn't want to spend time with the worker driving the four miles to Mosquito Creek to show him the right boat—big mistake. I told Russell the boat he was painting was a twenty-four-foot wooden boat, the third one on the left past the marina office. After two days, he realized he'd been working on the wrong boat, but was so worried that he phoned Louise to tell her instead of me. He had sounded so nervous that she felt sorry for him and told me not to be too tough on him. Russell had sanded and was painting the *fourth* boat past the office—a twenty-six-foot wooden boat. I was unhappy with Russell for not listening, but more so with myself for cutting corners.

"Paint the rest of it as quick as you can and pretend you're French or something if anyone talks to you." We raced to complete the job and quickly started painting the right boat. I wondered if the guy with a sparkling new, unplanned paint job ever noticed.

<><><>

Mr Rogers was a friendly guy—an ideal customer. We launched his thirty-foot powerboat in Cates Park, about a thirty-minute drive from our shop. It slipped nicely into the water from Bob's trailer. Joe, my mechanic at the time, cranked the engine over. Nothing happened. He kept cranking and cranking, over and over with no result.

We started to drift away from the ramp. I grabbed a paddle from the dinghy, jumped onto the swim grid and feverishly started to paddle the heavy vessel towards the dock. Joe couldn't help. He was recovering from back surgery. There was only one paddle, so Mr Rogers couldn't help either. After ten minutes of panicky paddling, the heavy vessel reached the dock and Mr Rogers jumped off and tied up the boat.

Joe continued cranking the engine. When not followed by the hearty roar of the V8 engine, it made a lonely sound that echoed mournfully across the inlet.

Could it be an air lock in the fuel supply?

Joe started checking the engine. Good-natured Mr Rogers filled in the silence by saying how peaceful it was without the engine running. After forty-five minutes, we all ran out of things to say as the boat rocked quietly at the dock and Joe sweated over the engine. An hour and a quarter after the launch, the deep rumble of the V8 breathed life back into the boat.

To fire up a boat engine in the shop was a pain: We had to rig up a cooling water supply instead of seawater, and an exhaust hose to the outside so as not to fill the shop with carbon monoxide. After the experience with Mr Rogers, it was a pain I always lived with.

I made many repair mistakes over the years, but usually only once. Mistakes often left me feeling worthless, sick to my stomach, and wondering if I should be in business. The journey from being an employee to becoming responsible for running a successful boat repair business was a long boulevard of learning—lined with humility.

I also made people mistakes, sometimes when hiring employees. Sid the mechanic interviewed well and came with great credentials. He was a certified Mercruiser mechanic and I happily displayed his certificates on the engine shop wall. Three weeks later, after installing two new Chrysler hemi engines on Mr Matti's thirty-foot Donzi powerboat, he forgot to put oil in them, and destroyed two $3,000 engines. Mr Matti lived on Passage Island and needed the boat to get back and forth to his house. He was livid at the delay.

I hired people who stole equipment from me, showed up for work inebriated, tried to do private work for my customers, or borrowed equipment and wrecked it. John, the apprentice, borrowed the company truck to launch his boat. He submerged the truck on the launch ramp—blamed his girlfriend who was driving and never told me for three days.

As well as making mistakes with employees, I also annoyed marine surveyors, aggravated subcontractors, and upset boat owners, or worse, their wives.

The worst customer's wife I irritated—or just added to an underlying irritation—was married to Bill, an affable, older radio host. The day before his twenty-eight-foot Bertram was scheduled to leave the shop, his wife appeared.

"Nice to meet you, Mrs Hawkes," I said, holding my hand out to greet her; she walked by me onto the boat. She was in her mid-sixties, hawk-nosed, blonde, and wearing a dark pantsuit.

"We've just finished replacing everything damaged by the sinking," I said.

Maybe she was a little deaf. She ignored me and silently surveyed the boat's interior—the new cushions, instruments, carpet, and re-furbished teak. She turned her gaze toward me.

"You haven't finished until I say you've finished." Her ice-blue, confidence-evaporating eyes bored into mine. I looked away.

"I don't like the headliner," she said, "It's dirty."

I explained that the headliner, the vinyl fabric lining under the cabin "ceiling," hadn't been submerged and that the surveyor would only approve what was damaged in the sinking.

"Maybe you should have been here when we were going over the repair specs," I suggested.

Her lips tightened. The icy eyes drilled into me once more, dispelling all doubt as to who was in charge.

"I want the headliner *replaced*," she said. "Phone my husband when you've done it." She lifted her chin and walked off the boat an out of my shop.

The surveyor phoned later that day. "I just talked to Mrs Hawkes about the headliner, Rod."

"Yeah, and how was that for you, Jim?"

"It was, em, like being dumped on by a water bomber on a cold day."

"Yeah. She's a lot scarier in person."

"I can imagine. Go ahead and replace the headliner. The world would be a calmer, happier place if you could do it by Friday."

I had assumed the quality of my relationship with boat owners would be commensurate with the quality of repairs to their boats, but found this to be incorrect. It was the owner's *perception* of the job that counted, not the actual work. An owner's understanding of quality could be turned negative by elements outside my control, sometimes by a friend in the pub.

We had been asked to repair a twenty-eight-foot plywood trimaran which had been damaged by an impact from a larger vessel as it lay moored at Coal Harbour. Fourteen-feet of hull on the starboard side needed replacing. I couldn't get the boat out of the water at Lynwood Marina because it was too wide for the slings. I got Bob, the boat mover, to haul it out at Cates Park, about four miles from the shop. My worker, Bob, agreed to sleep on the boat to protect it against theft. We used a portable generator for the power tools. The plan was to replace the two damaged sheets of plywood and sister five broken frames. After two days of work, Bill, the surveyor, phoned and informed me that the owner wanted us to stop work because he was unhappy with our repair methods.

"What do you mean, unhappy?"

"I don't know. Phone him up and ask him."

I was annoyed. It was difficult to work at Cates Park as it was, trucking all the materials out there, having someone sleep aboard to safeguard it from theft, and now the owner was complaining? I reached the owner by phone.

"Hi, Keith. It's Rod. The marine surveyor says you're unhappy with repairs?"

"Yeah, you're just patching the boat."

"How do you mean, just patching it?"

"You're just putting plywood patches on. My friend Wayne looked at it and said you're just patching it. I want it fixed properly."

I tried to bend my head around his thinking and reassure him. "There is no such thing as a twenty-eight-foot-long sheet of plywood, the builders of your boat used standard-length, eight-foot sheets of plywood," I explained. "In one way, your friend is right, we are putting patches on, but from that perspective, your whole boat is built of eight-foot patches. What does your friend do for a living?"

"He sells cars."

"I see. Maybe he doesn't know much about boats then? There are two ways of moving forward on this, Keith. We can either quit work on your boat today, and you can pay me for what we've done as per the work order you signed, or we can finish the job and re-launch it by Friday." A long pause followed.

"I guess you can continue."

I was usually more polite, but I had my limits.

Not all phone calls ended in work. Some people just had questions about their boats and I usually tried to help—not everyone could be helped—even with good intentions. I had a memorable conversation with a guy who was building a powerboat on Annacis

Island.

"Hi, My name's Fred. We need some help building a boat."

"What do you need help with?"

"We're building a forty-two-foot plywood powerboat, see? We done pretty good so far. We started at the back and worked forward. It was okay in the beginning because it was square at the back, but we're having a few problems now we're gettin' to the front."

"Did you loft it first?"

"What's that?"

"You draw the lines out full-size and make sure they are fair, so you don't have problems building the boat—especially the *front*."

"No, we didn't bother with all that. Em, look, I don't wanna spend a long time talking about it. Can you come out and help us or not?"

"Thanks, no. Annacis Island is too far. But, good luck."

Another caller phoned and started sobbing; she was much easier to help. "My boyfriend made me a canoe eight years ago, just before he was killed in a car accident."

"Sorry to hear that. How can I help you?"

"It's all cracked now, all over. It never used to be." More sobbing.

I waited. "Could you tell me what it's made of?"

"Wood. Cedar wood. He was a native carver, my Billy. He made it all from one tree."

I was getting the picture. Billy had made her a dugout canoe from a cedar tree. "Where do you keep it?"

"My son put it in the basement."

"Okay, here's what you do. Get your son to put it in the backyard and put about eight inches of water in the canoe with a garden hose. I think it's just dried out and cracked the wood. Don't store it inside. You should never keep a dugout canoe in the basement."

"Really? Oh, thanks. Thanks so much, sir."

"No problem. Phone me in a week if it's still cracked."

I never heard back.

Owning a boat enables visions of waterborne adventures. The boat repairer helps keep those dreams alive, but at what cost? The dichotomy of boat ownership is captured ruefully in the oft-quoted boat owner's reflection: *The two happiest days of a man's life are the day he buys a boat and the day he sells it.*

My accountant, Ed Waldheim, usually a placid, fifty-year-old bean-counter, phoned me one day, gleefully yelling down the phone line.

"Rod, I've finally sold my boat! I sold it to a friend. I gave him your number. He asked me if I thought he would like boating." Ed could hardly speak for laughing. "I told him if he liked standing in a cold shower flushing five-hundred-dollar bills down the drain, he would love boating."

In order to please boat owners, it's important to know what makes them happy, which is dictated by the kind of boating they do. I learned to recognise a few stereotypes:

Fish seekers — Nothing is as exciting as feeling a large salmon cranking on the line, bending your rod tip double. The vessel used could be anything from car-topper to forty-foot cruiser. The favoured lures varied from Lucky Louies, live herring, Hoochi-Koochies and Tom Macs, to buzz bombs, but fishing addicts never varied. They spared no cost for fishing equipment; they braved bad weather, spousal threats and cajoling from more successful cronies, but they never quit fishing. The tingle of a tugging rod had them hooked. They went boating to fish.

Romance seekers—Caught up by the romance of the sea, they bought a boat. After a few years of being drained by the high cost of moorage, maintenance and fuel, and using the boat much less than they thought, they were far more excited when selling the boat than when they bought it. These were often unhappy clients to deal with, because the cost and complexity of boating torpedoed their dreams of spending simple happy days on the water.

169

Commuters—Our clients living up Indian Arm were the least fussy about how their vessels looked. They were no-frills customers. As there were no roads to their homes, their only dream was to keep their boats running so they could get back and forth to work. A typical conversation went as follows.

"Hi, Billy here. My boat's at the dock—the eighteen-foot Hourston Glasscraft at berth 3A. Hard to start this morning. Kept backfiring, then spluttered under power."

"Sounds like the timing Billy."

"Whatever. Need it fixed by 5 p.m. Gotta go."

Indian Arm commuter boats were usually seventeen to nineteen feet long, banged up from daily dockings, the canvas tattered from the constant flap of whizzing through the water, and the engines well worn. The regulation life jackets, running lights, flares, balers, and paddles seemed optional on these busy runabouts.

Trophy boaters—At the other end of the scale were what I call trophy boaters. The pristine yachts moored downtown at the Royal Vancouver Yacht Club were like trophy wives—a demonstration of business success and virile masculinity. Often, the owners were too busy running their businesses to use their boats. To them, the thought of the boat waiting at the dock, just in case they had time to use it, was comforting—it reaffirmed who they were.

Sanctuary seekers—We rarely saw this breed. They took pleasure in doing all their own work and didn't want anyone else touching their pride and joy. "Took me three years, but I rebuilt the whole cabin by myself."

It was quiet down on the water, away from un-mowed lawns, wives, neighbours, kids, the phone, and other stressors. The boat was a private joy, a muse—still affirming the possibility of romance and adventure.

Adventure seekers—Savvy boaters who went places and got the most out of their boats each summer. If married, the family went with them. They knew how to avoid the many pitfalls of boating and were skilled navigators. With these customers, it felt like working with other professionals, so there were rarely any misunderstandings.

Wind seekers—Experienced sail boaters knew about the subtlety of wind, so they knew about the sea. Powerboaters could blast across the Georgia Strait, spend all day at Pirate's Cove and zoom back that evening, but you needed time and knowledge of the wind and water to get somewhere in a sailboat. Lots of schoolteachers owned sailboats. They had the long summer holidays—time to explore the coast.

Understanding boaters' needs was important for running my business. Running my business was a necessity in providing sustenance for my family, but as my sons grew older, sustenance didn't seem to be enough. Whereas I learned by experience to understand boaters' needs, I failed to understand what my sons needed. Their behaviour was becoming wayward, and they were getting into trouble—not so much at home, but at school and outside.

Louise and I took a parenting course together. I learned some useful ideas about parenting and put them into practice. I felt good about the learning, but not about the results—nothing changed.

I could still enjoy my daughter but in a different way, not the rough and tumble I had with my sons. We would sometimes go on walks together, pick wild flowers and arrange them in vases around the home.

I loved being a dad when the boys were young and not acting out, but later it was my work that gave me a sense of accomplishment and pride. It felt good to help people, to fix their problems efficiently, charge a reasonable price, and get them back in the water so they could enjoy their boats. Most of my customers were decent people whom I respected.

Over the twenty years I was in business, there were just a handful of customers who were very challenging. These individuals remain imbedded in my memory—on the dark side of my brain.

23 - Rogue Repair

"The need for control comes from someone that has lost it."
— Shannon L. Adler

It was 1989, and the world was changing for the better. After twenty-eight years, the Berlin Wall was pulled down, Gorbachev was liberalising Russia, and it looked like democracy was coming to China as tens of thousands of people rallied for democracy in Tiananmen Square.

Things were improving in my company. I had survived the loss of my partner/mechanic. The economy had bounced back from the 1980-85 recession and people had money to spend on boat repairs. The company owned a fax machine and had recently bought a computer, but I wasn't sure how to use it.

Surviving in business for thirteen years had grown my competence and confidence so that most repair challenges were handled smoothly and routinely by the systems I had put in place. Every once in a while, a repair job arrived into my care that broke loose, slithered past the normal parameters of control, overwhelmed my resourcefulness, exhausted my resilience, and sucked me into a quagmire from which there appeared no escape. Roy's sixty-five-foot Hatteras sailboat was one such job. Thinking about it, writing about it, causes my chest to heave—even now.

Roy Stein had been manoeuvring out of his berth in the Fraser River, looking ahead but apparently not up. The tall mast of his sailboat snagged an overhead power cable. A huge jolt of electricity sizzled down the mast like a bolt of lightning and lit up every piece of metal in his boat. This had happened two months before I was asked by a marine surveyor to give him an estimate for repairs.

I got out of my car and walked towards the boat at Dease Island Marina. It appeared normal from the outside, except for a three-by-six-foot section of the hull below the water line, which had been almost blown off as the bolt of electricity whacked the bottom of the boat.

I mounted the rickety ladder, estimate sheet in hand. Walking from the cockpit into the cabin felt like descending into a giant barbecue. A smoky smell permeated the whole boat. I felt the hairs on my arms standing on end and my scalp started to tingle—the fiberglass hull acted like a giant capacitor, retaining static electricity from the giant electrical blast.

The once white headliner fabric was grey and smoky with several places burned through. Each piece of expensive electronic equipment was now housed in a blackened, distorted plastic shell. Marine water hoses, reinforced with an imbedded spiral of wire, had been blown apart by the current surging through them. I tried turning over the six-cylinder diesel engine manually, but it was seized. The wiring harness looked like a giant, charred spider web gripping the engine. The skeins of electrical wiring carrying power throughout the boat were a melted mess of plastic and copper. All the fine, teak cabinetry that had touched any metal was scorched. The beautiful vessel, once someone's pride and joy, had been savaged by the massive bolt of electricity.

I pulled up a seat storage-locker cover and saw what had been a case of twelve Cherry Cokes—each can a perforated sieve. A pool of brown liquid lay at the bottom of the locker. The sweet smell had attracted a horde of ants, which were crawling busily around the sugary brown liquid. I slapped the lid shut.

My pen scratched on the paper, trying to record and describe all the damage. I filled up four sheets of foolscap. I put a dollar figure for the cost of material and the number of hours it would take:

Wiring: $1,300 materials— 68 hrs labour
Woodwork: $340 materials—130 hrs labour
Replace burned hoses: $290—thirty hrs labour
Replace headliner: $190 materials—sixteen hrs labour

The list was about five pages long and only a *'guestimate'* of course, but a start, based on what I saw in front of me. The big-ticket items, like the Raytheon radar unit, I would price by phoning the supplier.

I estimated every job that came into the shop, so it was familiar territory, except I had never repaired a boat whacked by a jolt of high-voltage electricity, but all the damage seemed visible, so I wasn't worried.

The marine surveyor assigned to this job, Terry, would also write a list of specs, which I and other repairers would quote on. Writing my own list worked well. I could add pricing while looking at the job. Curiously, the anchor winch, the propane barbecue from the aft deck, and the main electrical panel inside the boat had been removed. There was an eighteen by thirty-inch hole where the panel had been, and all the wires had been snipped off. Could be a problem—with the panel and labels missing, there was no indication of which items the wiring had powered—a challenge for the electrician. An expensive, uninstalled hi-fi radio system and speakers sat on the galley table and remained unharmed.

I wrapped up my estimate, jumped in my car, turned on 650 Easy Listening, and started the long drive back to North Vancouver. I was interested in the job. At $56,000, it was the second largest repair I had bid on. Big jobs were always welcome—they provided a large security blanket of work. In the winter when we weren't busy, I would bid lower to get the job. In the summer, I'd tender higher because we didn't need the work, but if we got it, the higher price would help compensate for the extra stress of being busy. Early April fell between seasonal extremes; we should finish just before entering our peak period of July. I wouldn't adjust the bid higher or lower, just base it on the actual estimated hours of labour, and material.

A week later, I submitted my estimate. Eight days after that, Terry phoned to say I'd got the job. Yippee! All my hard work had been worthwhile. I set up a meeting with the surveyor right away. I needed to ensure we would receive two interim payments—$20,000 and $40,000 at a third and two-thirds of the way through the repair—or my company would run out of funds. My suppliers needed paying every thirty days and my staff bi-weekly.

Terry phoned again. "About that sailboat. Can you arrange for it to be moved to Lynwood Marina close to you? The owner hasn't paid the storage bill. The insurance company doesn't want it seized, so they want you to pay the storage and moving costs. Just tack it onto the bill."

We got the boat towed to Lynwood Marina and I went aboard for a second time. I tried to get the owner to meet me, but he wasn't answering his phone. We couldn't start work till he had signed the work order. Damn, the clock was ticking and each day on dry land, or on 'the hard' as it was known, cost money. We needed to get going before the summer crush of work hit us.

"I can't get the owner on the phone," I told Terry, "Do you have another number for him?"

"No, only one. He's hard to get. Maybe he's out of town."

"Out of town? He has to sign a work order before we can do anything."

"Yes, I realize that. I will try him again."

"Do you have an address for him?"

"I'll go to his file and get it for you."

"Thanks, Terry. The sooner we get started the better."

The excitement of getting the big job evaporated, like being handed a birthday present, opening the box, and finding it empty. The plans I had for repair were put on hold. Feeling restless, I went back aboard the sailboat when it arrived at Lynwood Marina. Using a small hand pump, I transferred all the Cherry Coke from the locker into a bucket and emptied it in the gravel outside. The ants would be disappointed.

I brought Mike from Reed Electrical to look at the job and give me an estimate. He figured seventy hours. That was good; my estimate was only two hours less. I paid Mike $25 an hour and the shop rate was $50 an hour, so I could make good money on the wiring, if we ever got started.

A week later, feeling frustrated and unable to reach the owner by phone, I took the unusual step of going to his home address. I knocked on the door of his False Creek condo at 7 p.m. After the second knock, the door opened a crack and a soft, female voice asked me what I wanted. "I'm here about Roy's boat. I'm the repair guy."

My message was relayed back. "Why have you come here?" asked the hidden voice.

"I can't get Roy on the phone."

"Wait a minute." The door closed and opened a crack a few minutes later. "How did you get this address?"

"From his insurance company."

She relayed the message. I heard a low male voice in conversation.

"He will meet you aboard the boat tomorrow at 11 a.m."

"Okay. Tell him it's been moved to Lynwood Marina."

The following day I went aboard ten minutes early, just in case. At 11.20, just as I was about to leave, Roy showed up. He was medium height, in his late thirties and balding. His expression was blank as I held out my hand.

"Rod Baker, General Boatworks. We were the successful bidder on repairing your boat and I wanted to meet you to discuss repairs and get the work order signed."

"I don't want the fucking thing repaired. I wanted the insurance company to pay me out."

"Sorry to hear that. I didn't know."

"Yeah, you wouldn't know. They refused to pay me out, which is stupid. Why wouldn't they do it?"

"I don't know. I guess they have their own logic."

"Your estimate could go higher, right? It could end up costing them more."

"Yeah, if something is not on the surveyor's specs, it—"

"Well, I have no fucking choice. I'm never gonna use those bastards again. Give me the work order."

I passed it over and he signed, with an angry flourish, without reading it.

"The anchor winch, barbecue and electrical panel are missing."

"Yeah, they were stolen at the other marina."

"Could you tell me what items were hooked up through the missing electrical panel?"

"Can't remember. You figure it out. You're the repair guy." He turned on his heel, left the cabin and descended the ladder. It was the first and last time I saw him.

The meeting left me perturbed, but no matter; I had the precious work order signed and could legally proceed with the repair. I would be paid for the interim invoices and would put a mechanic's lien on the boat when it was completed to ensure the final payment. The mechanic's lien was written into the small print on the work order. No one reads the small print.

I set the reconstruction wheels in motion. Two woodwork guys started replacing the burned teak cabinetry, the electrician worked on repairing the damaged wiring, Kevin replaced the damaged hoses and fittings, Bob got on with repairing the hull damage, and the mechanic began pulling the engine apart to see what was wrong.

I was worried about the engine repair. It was too deep in the boat to pull out, which we normally did for rebuilding. I hadn't had the mechanic long and wasn't yet confident in his abilities. Malcolm was twenty-eight, had black hair down to his shoulders, and avoided looking me in the eye; he was my fourth try at finding a good mechanic since my partner, Paul, had left. His lack of eye contact had me wondering if he was using drugs.

"Do you think you can fix the engine in the boat, Malcolm?"

"Yeah, shouldn't be a problem."

I wondered how he could say that when it had been hit by mega-volts of electricity. Maybe the pistons were welded to the cylinder walls.

"Okay, let me know when you have the head off and have figured out why it's seized."

"Sure. Shouldn't be long."

I started pricing and ordering all the equipment for the boat— engine gauges, depth sounder, VHF radio, radar, 8D batteries, barbecue, electrical panel, anchor winch, etc. As the parts arrived, I stacked them neatly in the corner of my office. The pile was building.

Terry phoned and asked me if we could add the price of painting the hull of Roy's boat to the estimate. It had to be towed back after the accident and the hull had been scraped a lot.

"Painting a sixty-five-foot boat is going to cost around $12,000." I could hear him gasp.

"Really, that much?

I explained that a scaffold needed to be erected around the boat and every nick and scratch in the hull repaired. Then the whole hull needed sanding with 150-grit sandpaper, masking off and spraying with an epoxy primer. When the primer had dried, the hull would be sanded again with 320-grit sandpaper and sprayed with a topcoat of crosslinking, high-gloss polyurethane.

"Yes, I see, Rod, a big job indeed. Let me get back to you on that."

I suspected that Roy had insisted on painting the boat so it would boost the repair cost and make it more likely that the insurance company would pay him out. I didn't want to paint the hull. It was too risky: One paint run on the topcoat meant sanding the whole thing and repainting. You cant patch-paint high gloss polyurethane. As it was outside, a car driving by quickly could stir up dust which would stick to the fresh paint. With such a large job, we could get overspray on other boats in the marina. Painting a boat that big, especially outside, was fraught with risk. If we had to paint it, I would leave it to the very end so the weather was warmer. Terry phoned a few days later and confirmed that we had to paint the hull. The job was getting bigger.

Monday morning, April 16, 7.30 a.m. I walked into the office as usual, but there was something unusual—something missing. The big pile of materials and equipment for Roy's boat was gone. Dazed, I looked around the back of my desk—nothing. I scanned the shop floor in vain.

The pile of equipment hadn't changed locations by itself. Someone had come in overnight and stolen everything I had stockpiled in my office. I cursed out loud three or four times—$8,000 worth of equipment, gone. It felt like a punch in the stomach—no, a horse-kick in the stomach.

Speaking of horses, it was time to close the stable door. After phoning the police, I phoned an alarm company to get a price on installing a security system in the building and erected metal bars across the inside of the window—to discourage further thefts. I phoned my insurance company but they informed me we were only covered for theft of shop equipment, or equipment stolen from boats, not uninstalled boat equipment sitting on the floor.

I was really fed up. If we made ten percent profit on each job, we had the potential to make $6,500 on Roy's boat, but with the equipment stolen, I was already $1,500 in the hole and I hadn't even completed the job yet.

When I examined both front and back doors, there was no sign of forced entry. It looked like an inside job. Great, not only was I responsible for running the business, but now I had to sit down at coffee breaks at the same table with someone who had stolen $8,000 of equipment from me. It felt like everybody was winning in the boat business except me. I strained to please owners and surveyors with the best quality work and always paid suppliers and workers on time, but when I went home at night to get away from it all and dropped my vigilance, I got robbed.

As usual, I sat down and had coffee with the guys. It was my way of touching base with them. There were seven employees. Sitting where I could see everyone's faces, I dropped the bomb.

"All the stuff for Roy's boat was stolen last night. Must have been someone with a key as there was no sign of entry damage. Anyone know anything about this?" I stared carefully at each face, but never got an inkling of whom the culprit might be. They all looked uncomfortable.

Maybe it wasn't an inside job.

It would be preferable to think that, rather than looking for hidden clues among my workers.

A policewoman showed up the next day but seemed rather lethargic about doing anything more than taking a few notes.

"Are you going to dust for fingerprints?" I asked.

"I don't think that would be helpful."

"Why not?"

"It usually isn't."

I waited till the alarm company had installed the alarm before buying any more equipment. About a week later, Rich informed me he was quitting. He was twenty-three, short with dark hair, a little chubby and had only worked for me for a month. He explained that he and some friends had decided to drive to the Rockies and do some hiking. From there, they'd take their time driving back to Ontario.

"Nice that you can afford it."

"We saved up some money."

"When were you thinking of leaving?"

"Tomorrow."

"You're not giving much notice."

"No, sorry. We just decided at the last minute."

I was glad Rich was going. I didn't know him that well. I had hired him just for Roy's boat. Did his sudden departure mean he had stolen the equipment? I couldn't prove it, but I wanted to believe it. That way I wouldn't have to spend every day at work in a climate of suspicion.

When Bob had repaired the bottom damage to the sixty-five-foot Hatteras, it was ready for antifouling paint. I had just the guy—my son Mike. At fifteen, he had decided he didn't want to go to school any more. I had never been crazy about school myself, so didn't give him too rough a time. He had been to three schools already and got asked to leave two of them for fighting. It's easy to get misguided when you are young. I would offer him a taste of work and pay him by the hour—treat him fairly, the same as any other employee. I gave him a choice of school or paid work. I was adamant he couldn't just hang out at Circuit Circus on Lonsdale all day, playing video games. He chose work.

We set out at 7.15 a.m. It felt good to be going to work with my son. One day, maybe the whole family would be involved in the business. I also thought he would learn some lessons about work and money. He was very slow at painting, pasted quite a lot on himself as well as the boat, but finally got the hang of it. His white coveralls were pretty well covered in red antifouling paint by the time he finished the job. It took him a day and a half and I paid him six dollars an hour in cash. I think he was kind of surprised at the tediousness of work, but being resilient, stuck with it. After the work experience, he decided to go back to school.

The day after he returned, the electrician reported that all the expensive hi-fi radio equipment was missing. I phoned Roy, hoping he'd taken it for safekeeping, but he assured me he hadn't.

"Don't you lock the boat up when you're finished?"

"Yeah, of course we do, Roy, but once in a while, the Marina is the target of thieves."

I contacted the police; they came a couple of hours later to accompany me to the boat. This young constable seemed keen. He asked lots of questions. How many staff did I have? Did any of them have drug or alcohol problems? How long had I known them? Where were the boat keys kept? The keys to Roy's boat hung on a nail in my office wall. There was no sign of forced entry to the boat. Another theft, and this time, it couldn't have been Rich. He had left town. Maybe he didn't steal the other stuff either. It was unsettling. I found myself watching my staff for unusual behaviours. I observed them as they walked through the door in the morning, as they ate their lunch and filled in their time books at the end of the day. What were unusual behaviours? I hadn't a clue, but looked anyway.

There was progress on the engine. Malcolm said it needed the injectors rebuilt, a new wiring harness, belts, hoses, oil pump impellor, gasket kit, thermostat, and a starter, but it seemed to have survived any severe damage to the engine itself.

"You sure, Malcolm? It's not about saving money; it's about doing it right.

"I think it'll be fine with those new parts. The engine turns over now. Not sure why it didn't when you tried."

I wasn't convinced, but we would hook it up to water and run it before we launched the boat. When you've repaired the engine and it doesn't work, the silence is deafening.

Apart from Roy's sailboat at Lynwood Marina, we had two leaking aluminum car-toppers, a nineteen-foot fibreglass runabout in for a transom replacement, and a twenty-six-foot Zeta which had blown up due to a gas explosion. I had three guys working in the shop and three on the sailboat.

Two weeks after the equipment went missing from Roy's boat, the electrician had to break the padlock on a cupboard in the forepeak to complete some wiring and found all the missing goods. I let the police know and they came down to look. They informed me they had evidence that my son Mike was the culprit, but wouldn't say why because it was part of another "ongoing investigation." They thought he had stashed it there and was planning to return later to pick it up when things had cooled down.

I was upset at the police for not telling me why they thought it was Mike, and also at my son, because it seemed likely that they were right. If true, it was a complete betrayal. I had accommodated his decision not to go to school and tried to instil some work-for-wage values in him. For my trouble, it seemed like I had been ripped off and humiliated. I arrived home that night and questioned Mike for a good half hour.

What on earth had gotten into kids these days? Where was the respect? To make matters worse, he never admitted it which created an element of doubt. Things were pretty tense at home for a while.

My biggest fear was that Roy would find out. I would feel completely incompetent due to the allegations that my own son was responsible. I just wanted the whole thing to go away. When we found the hi-fi radio equipment, I phoned Roy to let him know the good news.

"Yeah, I heard your son stashed my stuff. Is that right?"

I died inside. "Well, unfortunately he may have, but no charges have been laid."

"What kind of operation are you running there? Your kid steals stuff from customers' boats?"

"My apologies. At least the stuff has been found. It won't happen again."

I collected my thoughts and tried to get back to work.

Despite Louise being a stay-at-home mum, my coaching their soccer teams for four years each and doing things as a family, both boys seemed to be on a disturbing downward trajectory, which led to them both to running foul of the law. It was the most heart-breaking experience. Despite our best efforts, their nefarious activities became more frequent. I had my work to distract me, but Louise didn't, and often became depressed over their behaviour.

Regardless of life at home, the relentless pace of summer was building. We rode into May at a trot, cantered through June, and entered July at full gallop with a shop full of boats.

Awaiting urgent repair, was a twenty-four-foot Starcraft needing the bowstem replaced, a twenty-six-foot Carver with a damaged bottom, a thirty-two-foot Uniflite which had suffered a fire, a twenty-foot aluminum river boat with leaking rivets, a burnt ship's lifeboat to be rebuilt, and a twenty-two-foot Bell Boy needing a transom replacement.

My mind creaked under the load as the shop hummed with activity. I was spinning plates like a circus performer, just able to reach them before they fell flat. At the end of the day, I drove home on the low road by the train tracks, weary and almost in a state of mental collapse. The *whazzam* of trains, shunting fifteen feet adjacent to the road, slapped me out of my torpor and made me sit bolt upright at the wheel. But by the time I had reached home ten minutes later, I had slumped down in my seat again.

I hired three new workers, for a total of nine. I was still bidding on boats, trying to take advantage of the heady summer pace before the phone stopped ringing in mid-September. Boats flew in and out of the shop as fast as we could repair them, but in the background, as always, unending since April as we edged into August, was Roy's sixty-five-foot sailboat—a steady drain on manpower and equipment.

We were almost done, everything inside was looking good, even the engine seemed to run well. The last thing was to apply the super-glossy polyurethane topcoat. It had to be done on a sunny day. We planned to start about 10 a.m. when the hull had warmed a little, but no later, as we needed to be finished by 3 p.m. The temperature had to be seventy degrees Fahrenheit and humidity less than sixty-five percent. If we finished any later, the temperature would be too cool and the air too humid, which would dull the finish of the paint. We would spray on three coats. At forty-five minutes per side, an hour and a half for the whole boat times three, meant four and a half hours of straight painting—an endurance feat. I gave Ravi a helper to move the compressor and hoses as he walked around the scaffold spraying the paint onto the hull.

An hour after Ravi started painting, the helper came running into the shop.

"Ravi said the job's going wrong and that you gotta come and look right away."

Going wrong was the last thing I needed; it would mean a huge cost overrun in time and materials, plus, in the open environment of the marina, everyone could see.

I shot over to the marina three blocks away. On the section Ravi had sprayed, hundreds of tiny bubbles were forming. I thought maybe oil from the compressor was getting into the paint, but checked and we had installed a fresh oil trap. The bubbles didn't appear until thirty minutes after spraying.

"Should I keep spraying?"

"Yeah, keep spraying." I said, because I didn't have another plan.

I walked down to Phil at Fraser Fibreglass and discussed the problem with him. He hadn't experienced anything like that before, but had heard of a case whereby the jolt from the high-tension wires was thought to have created minute voids in the fibreglass. If this were the case, it would explain the bubbles. After the paint landed on the hull, the sun's warmth expanded the air in the voids, which formed tiny bubbles in the paint's surface.

I was in new territory, but theorized that maybe a couple of coats would seal over the voids. When the paint dried, we could sand over the topcoat and try painting again. It was a lot of unplanned work. I phoned the surveyor to let him know about the extra cost.

"Terry, we are just painting the hull of Roy's sixty-five-foot Hatteras and there is a problem. Hundreds of bubbles are appearing in the paint."

"Why is that?"

"I don't know. It's never happened before." I explained the theory about electricity causing miniscule air pockets but he was not impressed.

"Rod, you are the boat repair expert. You quoted on painting, it was a lot of money, I agreed to the amount, but that's it."

"What about the air pockets causing the bubbles?"

"I've never heard of that before."

I could understand Terry's point. I had never heard of it either. It was hard to push a point I hardly believed in myself.

Two days later, we re-sanded the whole hull with 320-grit sandpaper, wiped all the dust off with tack rags, and set out once again to spray the hull. I watched like a hawk at the *whoosh, whoosh* of paint Ravi was shooting onto the hull. The white paint in the sun burned my eyes, but—no bubbles. It was working. Ravi and I exchanged a gleeful high-five. Ravi continued painting and I went back to the shop in a good mood. As long as no cars drove by and made dust, and no bees flew into the paint, I was safe. The boat was finally going to be out of my hair.

I started totalling up the final bill. With the paint job and other extras the surveyor had approved, it was almost $70,000. I had been paid $40,000 and was still owed $30,000. The mechanics lien insured that the final balance was secured and I didn't have to rely on the owner to sign the proof of loss, although it would be faster if he did.

I submitted the final bill to the surveyor and mailed a copy to Roy. As usual, Roy never answered the phone. I left a message telling him the boat was finished and that he should inspect it, pay the deductible, sign the proof of loss, and take possession. I was relieved to be done with it. Big repair jobs were like black holes that sucked in men, money and materials. This job had sucked some of the life energy from me.

I was going to England for a week to attend my sister's wedding. I didn't usually take time off in the summer, but if my sister had found the right guy, I wanted to be there for her. It would be third time lucky for her and a nice break for me. When I got back, the boat would be gone.

My brief sojourn was enjoyable. I got to see lots of family at the wedding and liked my sister's new husband, an American Navy guy who worked on aircraft carriers. The visit passed quickly. I shook my new brother-in-law's hand, hugged my sister as they dropped me off at the airport, and was homeward bound.

The plane cleared the Rockies and settled on a shallow descent path as we passed over the Okanogan Valley, dropping down into the Fraser River delta. Not following the usual flight path, we flew over Port Moody and along the Burrard Inlet, just to the south of Lynwood Marina. Incredibly, while peering through the plane window, to my dismay, I saw Roy's boat still sitting in the yard. Wondering why the heck the owner hadn't picked it up, and who was paying for the extra storage, jolted me out of my holiday mood.

My anxiety overrode my jet lag. The plane arrived at 11 a.m. and I went straight to the shop. Kevin informed me that there was an official notice pasted on the boat. Apparently, the federal government had seized the boat under a relatively new law related to drug profits. Luckily, we had put a mechanic's lien on the boat. I phoned my lawyer, Jim Poyner, and asked him how to proceed.

"Your lien is provincial, Rod. The seizure notice is federal. Federal cases trump provincial cases."

"So, what will happen here? Will I get my $30,000?"

"Can't tell you for sure. It's a relatively new law so there are few case precedents."

This was the last straw. First, I had to deal with a recalcitrant, non-appreciative owner, the theft of equipment from my office, my son probably trying to steal the radio equipment, the paint job going wrong, the surveyor not accommodating my paint bubble theory, and now the damned boat had been seized by the federal government. I stomped around the shop cursing for ten minutes and then went into the storage room, grabbed a distress flare, went outside and fired it off. The whooshing sound, acrid smoke, and flaming rocket spiralling skyward gave me some relief.

About six months later, six months of worry, I received a $30,000 cheque from the insurance company—the final amount owing. It was a satisfying feeling, popping the final payment cheque into the bank deposit box on my way home from work. The *click-clunk* of the deposit box opening and closing signalled a banal, normal end to a scary, abnormal job. I wanted to believe I broke even on the job. Probably I didn't, but at least the money owed had been recovered— my mind never did.

I started to think about new ways of making money—selling things. Repairs were too difficult. Selling things must be easier. You ordered stock, people dropped by the shop and bought the product. No repairs needed. It was a clean solution to earning money with less worry, hassle, and risk. I needed something related to my business— outboard motors maybe. They were big-ticket items. Yes, I could visualise it. Customers would come to my shop for repairs, see a lovely selection of outboard motors, and buy one. I decided to become an outboard motor dealer.

24 - Inside Outboards

'Go out on a limb. That's where the fruit is."
— Jimmy Carter

I hate pushy salesmen. I have a slow mind. I look at something I'm buying for a long time, just getting a feel for it, getting my head around it before questions come. When salesmen approach and tell me the answers to the questions before I've thought of them, I want to leave. I want to think of my own questions.

I was going to become a salesman, but not that sort of salesman. *You can't be someone you don't like, not every day.*

Selling things was a new idea for me. It was going to be easy—easier than repairs. You didn't need to fix anything. You bought stock, marked it up, and sold it. No dust, no smell, no risk. No one complained about your work.

I was already in the boat business, so outboard motors seemed like a natural fit. Small boats needed outboards, medium size boats often used outboards for trolling, and large boats had dinghies with outboards.

But which outboards should I sell? Or, a more pertinent question, which manufacturer would have me as a dealer?

I wasn't a mechanic and had never sold outboards or anything else. I noticed a new brand of outboard advertised in Pacific Yachting—Nissan Outboards. They were probably looking for dealers. Maybe we could be new together. I checked around and found the only other Nissan dealer was in New Westminster, two cities away. Great—I didn't want to compete with someone close by who knew what they were doing.

I found the phone number of Nissan headquarters in Toronto and talked to someone called Jack. We discussed my becoming a dealer. He liked the fact that I was in the marine business and owned the building, but seemed surprised about the lack of outboards in my life.

"You've never sold outboards before?"

"No."

"But you have an outboard mechanic?"

"No, I don't—not yet."

"We need to meet, Rod."

He suggested I come to Valleyfield, Quebec to meet him and attend a dealers' meeting. Surely, I wouldn't go all that way to be refused. Maybe that was the test.

I had always operated as a lone wolf. Now, maybe, I was going to be part of the Nissan family. I would fly across the country to the meeting. Travelling for business sounded cool. I had always envied other such folks. Usually, the farthest I got to travel was to do an estimate at Lions Bay, twenty-five kilometres away. On this trip, I had to pay for the flight and the hotel. Never mind—it would be worth it, probably.

Jack met me in the conference room of the Hotel Valleyfield. He was fortyish, slim, and dressed in a dark suit. His outstretched hand was cold to touch.

"Welcome to the Nissan outboard dealers' meeting, Rod," he said, with a flicker-smile, before turning back to some paperwork.

There were about twenty-five dealers from across Canada at the two-day meeting. I was the only guy from the West Coast. They all knew one another. Some were friendly others ignored me. I didn't talk much. I couldn't think what to say.

The morning was spent discussing the new outboard models that would soon be available, and answering dealers' questions. It was educational. Some of the dealers got quite snippy about perceived injustices. One guy in a plaid shirt from Newfoundland suggested that, as Nissan was a new brand, the dealers should get compensated for advertising because they were helping increase Nissan brand recognition. Everyone applauded.

Jack's cool demeanour remained unruffled. He explained that Nissan would unveil a national marketing plan by the next dealers' meeting.

"If there's any of us left by then, boy," quipped the 'Newfie,' to muffled sniggers.

In the afternoon, we gathered in the same conference room. A

190

sales expert gave us a pep talk about something called *target marketing*. If we did what the expert said, we could increase sales. It felt good to be part of a team, even if I didn't understand much about target marketing. It seemed too aggressive. I learned that I was supposed to have a sales strategy because "Outboards don't sell themselves."

I learned that Nissan also sold inflatable dinghies. It made good sense to sell them as a package. Having a showroom full of inflatable boats with engines mounted on them would look pretty cool—more realistic, Jack said. He also promised to show us how to repair Nissan inflatable boats. Good, I liked the idea of learning neoprene repair techniques—it increased the range of hulls we repaired.

Next day, the Nissan Marine vice president, Ace Ishikawa, showed up fresh from Japan to address us. This was the first time most of the dealers had seen him. Jack told us it was a big deal; he rarely made an appearance in Canada. The dealers hushed as he entered the room, a diminutive figure in an olive-green suit and spectacles. He reached the podium and, in stilted English, read doggedly from a script without looking up. He told us it was an honour for him to be in Canada and an honour to be in the presence of so many hard-working dealers—that we were all doing a great job ... my mind began to wander at this point.

I wasn't used to meetings. I was getting bored, drifting away, feeling sleepy. I wondered if Ace was his real name. It didn't seem Japanese. Maybe it was a character in an American movie he had liked—maybe a hustler or a card shark. What was I doing in Quebec, listening to some Japanese guy talking about honour and outboards? Oh, well, I was stuck here now. I dozed off briefly.

It was official. Jack invited me into a small office and presented me with the dealership contract. Prior to the dealers' meeting, it hadn't occurred to me that sales might be a problem because people didn't know that Nissan made outboard motors. I had assumed name recognition would cross over from the cars and trucks they built. Not wanting to waste my trip to Quebec, I signed at the bottom of the fifteen sheets of paper Jack pushed at me, and became a Nissan outboard dealer.

I ordered ten outboards and four boats—a value of $19,000. Just the twelve-foot inflatable and twenty-five horsepower engine package retailed for close to $6,000. I hoped I could sell what I had ordered. Nissan would finance them until the end of the year, and then, whatever wasn't sold, I had to pay for. If half the stock wasn't sold in the next six months, I would have to ask the bank to increase my $10,000 revolving loan. If the economy didn't remain buoyant, target marketing or not, I would be in trouble.

I found out a few weeks later from Andy, a local Evinrude dealer, that Nissan didn't even make outboards; they just slapped Nissan stickers on outboards made by a company called Tohatsu. Sometimes, I just charged into things and figured out how to cope later.

I mulled over Nissan Outboard's lack of brand recognition on the plane home. Maybe I should also carry a well-known brand, like Mercury, in case the Nissans didn't sell. When I got back to Vancouver, I asked the opinion of my buddy Jim, at M & P Mercury Marine; he sold two brands of outboards.

Jim was a big, slow-moving guy I had done fibreglass work for over the years. He invited me into his tiny office crammed with engine parts and answered my question.

"Two brands? Don't do it, Rod."

"Why not? You do."

"I'll tell ya." He relaxed back into his battered leather chair and exhaled a long breath. "A guy comes in looking for an outboard. He wants to know all about the Merc. That takes ya twenty minutes. Then he asks about the other brand. So ya tell him all about the Mariner. That's another twenty. Then he walks around the showroom looking at the brochures, prodding and poking both brands for another ten minutes apiece. That's another twenty. You've spent an hour with him. But he gets confused about which one to buy and leaves without buying either."

"You're kidding."

"Nope. Drives me crazy."

Jim sold me. It made sense, or maybe Jim just didn't want another Mercury dealer around.

I built a showroom at the back of the shop ten feet above the floor, fifteen-feet wide and thirty-feet long, across the width of the shop. We erected a wall across the front of the showroom up to the ceiling, to keep the fibreglass dust out, and installed a big window overlooking the shop. My guys painted the interior walls a nice pastel blue and installed a light grey carpet on the floor. I bought a couple of original waterscape paintings from a local Dutch artist of sailboats at anchor—a tranquil scene. Finally, we made a hatch in the floor at one end with a winch above it, for hauling the larger outboards up and down.

The showroom looked smart, the best part of the shop. I couldn't wait to escort the first customer through the dusty, noisy shop and upstairs to the pristine showroom, full of brand-new Nissan outboards and inflatable boats. It was going to be great. Customers would stroll in, buy a package and increase our revenue—no repairs involved.

I phoned Jack to tell him I had built the showroom and wanted some engines. It turned out I wasn't ready.

"You're gonna need a set of microfiche sheets and a microfiche reader," he explained.

"What's a microfiche sheet?"

"A plastic sheet with all the outboard parts on. Nissan supplies them. You put it in the microfiche reader, which illuminates and magnifies the sheet." This was sounding complicated.

"Where do I get the reader from?"

"Try and get a used one—new are expensive. Then you'll need a supply of parts, numbered parts boxes to put them in, and outboard motor stands for the motors to hang on."

"We never discussed the need for all this stuff when I was signing the dealership papers." I had figured $20,000 for the start-up but the stock, the cost of building the shop, and now all this other stuff meant

I was running way over.

"It's obvious, isn't it?" said Jack.

It would have been, if I had known more about outboards.

"When we send you the parts, we'll include some Nissan Marine brochures. Stamp them with your company stamp and use them at boat shows or fax them to people making enquiries about Nissan products."

"Okay, thanks Jack."

"Last thing, Rod. You got MasterCard and Visa, right?"

"No, I don't."

"I advise you to get it. People don't walk in the store with a couple of thousand bucks in their pocket in case they buy an outboard. If they give you a bad cheque, you're screwed. That's why you need to accept credit cards," he explained.

I had never thought of that, but the way Jack put it, it sounded right. Jesus, more work. I picked up the phone and got busy learning about what I needed to do to accept credit cards.

Once again, I needed to find a new marine mechanic. They are an unusual breed, who have to deal with salt-corroded stern drives or replacing starter motors by wedging themselves under the engine, instead of having the luxury of working under a hoist as car mechanics did. I'd had difficulty finding someone reliable since my partner, Paul had left. Bad mechanics are dangerous to boaters and thus to my business. For the first few weeks after hiring a new mechanic, I held my breath and hoped none of the engines we'd repaired broke down or blew up and that all mechanical problems could be diagnosed and repaired.

Sometimes mechanics quit, or if they didn't work out, I laid them off. When we were between mechanics, it was unnerving. We could suddenly get three mechanical repairs come in and I'd have to hire someone right away—never good for quality control. My last mechanic, Malcolm, had been proficient, but then went missing. He didn't show up for work for a week, then I got a phone call from him explaining that his mother was dying of cancer and he had gone back to Ontario to look after her—and forgot to phone me.

I phoned Terry, the Nissan dealer in New Westminster, and asked him if he knew of any mechanics with Nissan Outboard experience. He told me he'd laid off a guy called Steve Queck, who might be interested.

"Why did you lay him off?"

"Winter. Not enough work."

"Is he okay?"

"Yeah, he's okay."

I didn't know Terry well and hoped he wasn't setting me up with a bad mechanic. It was a competitive business. Thinking about hiring a qualified Nissan outboard mechanic got me excited. In my mind, I had already hired him. Getting a mechanic familiar with Nissans would be a big bonus, but hiring any mechanic was tricky. Not being a mechanic myself, it was hard for me to evaluate their competence. Mistakes didn't show up until after you hired them. The hiring interview often consisted of me posing questions based on mistakes previous mechanics had made. It was a bonus if I liked the guy, but my focus was on hiring the most competent person possible. I phoned Steve. His voice was quiet. I couldn't get a sense of him.

"Have you ever used microfiche sheets?" I asked.

"Of course. How can you work without them? Do you have a microfiche reader?"

"I'm getting one. I'm just setting up the dealership. The parts are arriving in a couple of days."

He asked me more questions than I asked him, then finally agreed to come to the shop and take a look around. It was good that he was cautious, I told myself afterward.

Steve arrived in the shop a couple of days after our phone conversation. He was a short, Asian guy in his fifties from Singapore and wore a Nissan baseball cap. He shook my hand limply and looked around wide-eyed as I showed him the premises. I could see him taking it all in, trying to digest the situation. At his previous job with Otter Outboards, there had been two other mechanics, his boss Terry was a mechanic, and the focus had been solely on outboard motors. He wiped his finger on a flat surface and looked at the fibreglass dust.

I had more for him to consider. "We also work on inboards, stern drives, and occasionally diesels. Would that be a problem for you?"

"It shouldn't be. I can probably learn what I don't know if you get the manuals. Thanks for showing me around. How about I let you know in a couple of days?"

No one had said that before. They either took the job or they didn't. Maybe it was a polite way of saying "No." Maybe he was still looking around for something better, more familiar, less dusty.

He phoned three days later and said he might be interested if I offered him a couple of bucks an hour more. It went against the grain. I usually gave raises of fifty cents an hour, and this guy wanted a raise of two dollars an hour and didn't even work here yet.

"But I offered you what Terry was paying you."

"Yeah, Terry's been paying me that since I started there four years ago."

I was disappointed. You would think what I was offering was better than sitting at home doing nothing. It would cost me $16 a day more, but hiring Steve was the last big piece of the Nissan jigsaw puzzle I was trying to complete.

"Okay. I will pay you what you're asking. Can you come in next week?" I was all set, except for the microfiche reading machine.

Ten outboard motors and four inflatable boats arrived from Toronto along with four cases of outboard oil, $1,000 worth of engine parts, twenty life jackets, and ten paddles. Unwrapping everything was exciting, like Christmas, but instead of socks and shirts, it was outboard motors. The packing crates and cardboard almost filled my garbage container.

I had doubts about selling customers paddles. "Hey, you should buy a paddle. If the outboard I sold you quits, it'll come in handy."

These were the first brand-new outboards I'd seen up close. There was no smell of sea slime or two-stroke smoke, just a faint whiff of new metal. The lower casing of the motors was dark grey and the hoods that covered the engines were blue and silver-grey with a diagonal red stripe. Once they were mounted on stands, and on the boats we inflated in the showroom, the whole set-up looked fabulous.

I put an ad in the North Shore News announcing our new dealership. The ad cost over a hundred dollars, then I waited for the phone calls to start flooding in—nothing happened. Five days later, my first outboard customer dropped by. He was a slightly built guy wearing a blue baseball hat and jeans.

"I seen your ad in the paper for outboards. I'm lookin' for a twenty-five horse."

"Thanks for dropping in. I'll take you up to the showroom."

He followed me to the back of the shop, up the stairs, and stepped into my pristine showroom glistening with virgin outboards waiting to be courted by owners.

"I'm leaving for the cabin tomorrow. How much for this twenty-five horsepower here?"

"Eighteen-forty-five. There's a two year—"

"Okay, I'll take it. Can you pack it down for me?"

He had bought an outboard—my very first sale. I hadn't even used the target marketing sales technique. I couldn't remember it anyway. Unlike the marketing guy claimed, the outboard *had* sold itself. Could I pack it down? I was so energized, I could have packed an elephant down. I forgot about the winch and hatch I had installed for that purpose.

My hand was shaking as I filled out all the unfamiliar warranty documents. My customer paced around the office waiting for me to finish. It took twenty longer-than-normal minutes. I didn't want to make a mistake with my first customer, but I'd written the wrong year down. Luckily, Jack corrected it when I forwarded him the warranty papers.

"How would you like to pay?" I realized then that I should have asked this before I filled in the warranty papers.

Shit! Next time.

"MasterCard." I took hold of his card, loaded his card in the machine and put the papers on top as the MasterCard salesman had shown me last week. Saying a silent prayer, I snapped the slider back and forth over the whole caboodle. It seemed to work. I hoped so, otherwise the customer was leaving with a free $1,800 engine.

"Kevin, could you pack Mr Morris's outboard into his truck for him?"

After the customer left, I realized I had forgotten to offer him Nissan life jackets, Nissan Outboard oil, a Nissan paddle, and a spare propeller. No matter, I had sold my first outboard. I sat back in my office chair in silent satisfaction and had a cigarette. I was trying to quit, but I borrowed one from Bob. It was a worthy occasion. After all the work and expense of setting up the dealership, I had sold my first outboard. It had been easy—it was the easiest one I ever sold.

Three months later, my Nissan dealership was in full swing. I had sold five outboards and one inflatable boat. When customers phoned for parts, I could read the used Bell and Howe microfiche machine, fresh from the *Buy and Sell* paper, to get the part number and check the parts boxes to see if we had the required item.

I developed a sales technique, but it wasn't target marketing. Talking about how great Nissan outboards were was boring. No one bought an outboard because they liked them; they were a means to an end, frequently, to go fishing.

So I talked about fishing—a subject everyone loved, including me. We talked about bait, lures, the best spots to fish, the latest fish finders, how deep to fish, where to buy fishing tackle, and the best way to cook fish once they were caught.

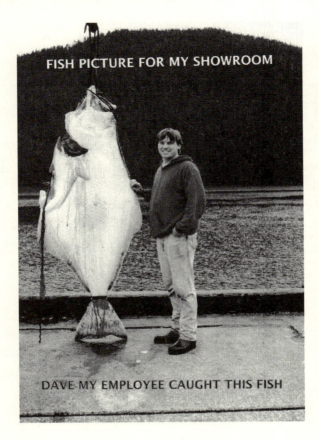

FISH PICTURE FOR MY SHOWROOM

DAVE MY EMPLOYEE CAUGHT THIS FISH

I put a few fishing pictures up on the wall and even got a couple of customers enthused who hadn't considered fishing.

After sharing our fish-catching experiences, secrets, and not discussing outboards, the customer usually brought the conversation back to the reason for their visit.

"Well, shall I buy this outboard or not?"

I responded casually and truthfully. "It's up to you. Most outboards are pretty similar, except that Nissan has a two-year warranty and all the others have one year."

I pointed out that selling outboards was not our main business, unlike Riverside Marine, which probably sold a hundred Mercury outboards a year. If they bought an outboard from us and it broke down, we'd be able to fix it right away due to our low volume of sales.

"If you lose two weeks of fishing time waiting in line to get your outboard repaired, that time is gone for good." It was a convincing argument.

Sometime later, I got a plaque congratulating General Boatworks for being one of the top ten Nissan outboard dealers in Canada. Even though there were only twenty-eight dealers, it felt gratifying. The dealership was working as I had hoped. Customers came in to buy outboards, saw that we did boat repairs, and had us work on their boat. Others came in for boat repairs, noticed we had Nissan products, and bought an outboard or inflatable boat.

I met a new range of people. A few German tourists bought inflatable packages. They often rented camper vans and went up to the Chilcotin, a wilderness plateau four hundred miles north of Vancouver. The inflatable packages were just the ticket—they could be packed in the camper, then inflated at the lakes for fishing.

I spent an hour in the showroom with an older visitor from Hamburg, Mr Krutzman. "Yah, I think I will take one package. They are good. But first I must check with the government."

That was confusing. I never knew the government had to be involved. "Which government, the Canadian or German?"

"The government in my house." We both laughed out loud. Even though we were different nationalities, we both had governments at home.

Another guy in his mid-thirties, already balding, had gone up to the showroom by himself because I was on the phone. He was sitting in a dinghy and staring into space.

"Thinking of going fishing?" I asked, offering the bait to get him talking. I didn't expect his answer.

"I'm thinking of pretending to go fishing."

"Pretending?" His answer had me baffled.

"I have a very stressful job in the movie industry. Last week, I had to find nine pre-war Harley Davidsons. One of the actors said he could ride, but then ended up throwing the bike down the road. Try explaining that to the owner!" He cursed a little, then carried on. "My time off is precious. I want solitude. People don't bother you when you're fishing. Hell, I don't even want to be bothered by fish."

He explained that last week he was fishing in Harrison Lake. A fisheries patrol vessel came by and the guy yelled across the water, "Are you using a triple hook?"

"I told him I'm not using any hook. He made me pull up my line and saw there was no hook, only a weight. He looked at me strangely, blinked, thanked me, and zoomed off muttering to himself."

"Yeah, no doubt," I said, picturing the incredulous fishery officer telling his colleagues about the crazy guy fishing with no hook.

The dealership was working well in other ways. My son Steve was nineteen and had been drifting around working at a variety of dead-end jobs, or just not working. I was worried about him. He was very bright, but couldn't seem to get hooked into life. As my mechanic Steve Queck was working out well, I suggested to my son that if he was interested in becoming a marine mechanic, I could offer him an apprenticeship. To my surprise and joy, he accepted. Maybe this would prove to be the right road at last.

I got him some extra-large coveralls and he came into work with me. The 7.30 a.m. start time was difficult, but he made it. They made an odd couple. Steve Queck was five-foot-two and my son six-foot-seven. They got on well together, and my son started to learn some basic mechanical skills. I was a happy dad.

Maybe Steve had turned a corner. Perhaps Mike would come and work here too; it could be a family business. Louise had said she didn't like the shop because it was dusty and dirty, but if the boys both worked here, maybe she would come. She could work in the showroom, maybe. It was clean up there.

After an eight-month stint as an apprentice marine mechanic, Steve left the shop one day to remove a carburettor from a boat in Deep Cove and never returned.

"I got fed up with all that work shit, Dad. It's too cold in the winter and kind of boring," he explained days later, when I finally caught up with him.

"So, it's over, just like that? I went through a lot of trouble to set up the apprenticeship for you. Where's the carburettor now?"

"I took it back to the shop. It must be there somewhere." I was sad, but we had both tried and it hadn't worked out.

The outboard dealership was another leap forward for the business. Like a giant macrophage, I had stretched myself around and swallowed all the requirements of becoming a dealer. We had a Nissan-trained mechanic and a showroom full of Nissan products. The Nissan dealership increased our revenue by about ten percent and gave us more visibility; exactly what Melvin, the Yellow Pages guy, had said all those years ago. My dislike of pushy sales talk had worked. Talking about fishing netted more customers than hosing them down with outboard facts. Jimmy Carter had been right: going out on a limb produced fruit.

The longer I was in business, the more I learned and the better results I achieved. I'd gone into business to provide for my family. It had worked financially, but understanding what was happening to our sons was tougher. Things felt out of control, not at all what Louise and I had imagined for them. It was wearing on us both. Much of our energy was taken up trying to deal with and correct our sons' behaviour. I had an idea that a break from it all would be good.

STEVE B AND STEVE Q TEST DRIVING A BOAT.

25 - The Great Escape
*"We must be willing to let go of the life we planned,
to have the life that is waiting for us."*
— Joseph Campbell

It was 1991, I was forty-four years old, and the world was improving. The Soviet Union had ceased to exist and the cold war had ended. Apartheid had been defeated in South Africa and Nelson Mandela was free. On the financial front, the Dow Jones topped 3,000 for the first time ever. Things were looking good for my business as well—I had reliable staff; the outboard dealership was up and running; and, most exciting, both the house and shop mortgages were paid off that year.

Fifteen years ago, I had started the business in order to pay the mortgage—now we owned our home and the 6,000-square-foot warehouse. I had shaken off the heavy burden of debt from my shoulders. I wanted to breathe free, reflect and celebrate.

It was a watershed year for another reason: My father had died aged forty-four, three years before I immigrated to Canada.

He had never met my wife and children, or seen my house and business. After marrying my mother when he was twenty-three, Dad had spent his life struggling to provide for his wife and four kids until he died of pancreatic cancer. Mum still lived in the bungalow that his hard work had paid for. I had reached that same age—forty-four. It spooked me to think I would soon exceed my father's age. How could that be? Dad had always been older, wiser, stronger.

His untimely death reminded me that life was uncertain. Now I had reached that landmark age, it prodded me to start thinking about enjoying life before it was too late—try to stop my work days whizzing by like dominoes toppling over, quit stressing over my sons' behaviour, stop worrying about employees, customers, and all the challenges of repairing broken boats. Louise and I should take a break and enjoy our remaining time on the planet. Maybe we could do it together as a family—have some time out to reconnect.

"Let's leave everything behind, take a year off and breathe some fresh air." I brought it up a few times. "We could stay with my sister

Alison to start, then buy a van and travel." Louise liked Alison.

"I'm not sure, Rod. It's a big change. I'll think about it."

Our sons' behaviour had been like ice water dripping onto our heads, ebbing away our confidence as parents and the joy of family. Our focus on the boys had taken time and energy away from Alexis.

At the time we discussed the trip, it was 1991, Steve was twenty, Mike sixteen, and Alexis was eight. By then, the police had been to our house so often they knew our golden retriever's name.

Louise was an honest soul—the kind of woman who, if she got a dollar extra in change at the Safeway checkout, would walk back into the store and return it so the clerk's till would balance. Our sons' behaviour disappointed us both. It wasn't what we had planned.

I thought back to my youth. Three things were banned at school—gambling, smoking, and transistor radios. A few of us used to sit behind a big pile of bricks listening to my transistor radio, playing cards for money, and smoking. In my experience, any teens worth their salt stretch limits—it's part of finding boundaries—but today's kids, our kids, seemed to have no respect for limits, and boundaries were casually ignored. They didn't seem to learn from mistakes. In my youth, if we got caught a couple of times doing something wrong, we quit, or at least, were a lot more careful.

The big vacation idea had been building in my head for about six months. Louise was coping better and the mortgages were paid. We could rent our house and have money for the trip. I would ask Kevin if he would run the shop. Steve hadn't lived at home for a couple of years. Louise, Mike, Alexis, and I, could go to Europe, hang out at my sister's place for a while, then buy a van and travel. I hoped it would do Mike good to meet some of his English relatives, and maybe get a different perspective on life. Alexis could meet her cousins, go to school in England for a few months, and then Louise could home-school her while we travelled in the van.

Maybe the change of country, scenery and circumstances would help us all. I kept telling Louise we needed a break, and she finally agreed. She found out about home-schooling and sent away for all the necessary books.

Sure, it was a little out of the ordinary leaving everything—the business, house, and our friends—behind, but life should include some adventure. We rented the house to a couple with a Great Dane who said they would look after our dog—great! Mike and I went to get his passport photos together. He didn't seem that excited and showed up late for the appointment.

Kevin agreed to run the business; he would pay rent to me and keep any profit he earned. I went down to the shop the day before we left to give Kevin a final briefing about which customers owed us money, what to do if we got too much work, whom to lay off if we got too little work, and a hundred other things. I gave him my sister's number in England, shook his hand, and wished him good luck. It was September, and for once I was happy that things were slowing down. Kevin wouldn't be too stressed. I felt good leaving everything in his hands. He was a rock-solid guy.

Although I had talked everyone into the idea, it still felt unreal and unstable walking away from the business I had poured my heart into for the last fifteen years and leaving our family home for someone else to live in.

Still, what's one year in a lifetime?

Too often the years merged together, one indistinguishable from the next. We would certainly remember our year away.

The big day arrived—September 15, 1991. We were packed and ready to go. Sophie, our dog, knew something was happening and lay across the threshold of the door. Mike had insisted on sleeping overnight at a friend's house, but had been told to be back by 10.30 a.m. We were leaving at noon. He never came home. We kept the cab waiting an extra ten minutes and then left. Feeling panicky, we assumed, we hoped, he would show up at the airport. We unloaded our cases and pulled them towards the Air Canada counter while scanning the crowds for his face. We couldn't see him. Maybe that's why he had wanted his ticket the day before, so he could pass through ahead of us and freak us out—Mike, always the joker! We reached the counter and Louise asked the flight check-in lady if Mike Baker had already been processed to board the flight.

"I have absolutely no way of knowing that, ma'am. Even if I did, it would be confidential."

"But he's our son," explained Louise. "We just want to know if he's ... if he came."

The attendant gave us a familiar *what incompetent parents* look. "Sorry, ma'am," she said, shaking her head and beckoning the next passenger to proceed.

There was only one way to find out. We would have to go through security and see if he was in the passenger lounge. Feeling conflicted, we passed through inspection and dragged our cases hurriedly toward the lounge, checking the shops on the way. He was nowhere to be seen. Maybe he was hiding out somewhere, showing his independence—typical. We sat down uneasily and waited.

"The Air Canada flight for Stanstead, London, is boarding now at terminal 28." No Mike in sight. As the last of the passengers went through the gate, we hung back, agonising about what to do. Should we leave without him? If we stayed, where would we live? Our house was just rented. What would I do, tell Kevin the deal was off after all the careful planning? The last of the passengers were filing past the attendant.

"Rod, do you think he slipped aboard somehow?"

It was a faint hope. We wanted hope.

"Sir, if you are catching this flight, you need to board immediately."

"Louise, let's get on the plane. He might be there, but either way, this is exactly the sort of thing we wanted a break from. If we don't get on, they will have to unload our baggage from the plane and hold up the flight."

Damn Mike, his seat was empty. We sat on the plane numbed and devastated at this latest betrayal. It added to the cumulative weight of all the past betrayals, one of the main reasons we were going away. We tried to be positive about our new venture and avoid looking at the empty seat beside us, but the sadness of leaving without Mike pervaded the air for the whole flight.

My sister, Alison, was quite shocked when we arrived without Mike. "What do you mean, he's not here?" It made us feel incompetent, as though we had somehow misplaced one of our children. At least it would be less crowded in her small cottage.

We lived with Ali for the first three weeks until we rented a quaint bungalow on a nearby farm. It had a small extra bedroom in case Mike showed up.

I kept in touch with work weekly by phone. Kevin was doing a great job. Our only concern was our missing son. The extended vacation had seemed viable until Mike no-showed. We knew he would survive. He was street-smart; he'd left home before for a couple of months when he was fourteen and stayed with friends. His survival wasn't the point. We had hoped this trip would help him see things differently—encourage better behaviour, not provide another opportunity to go astray.

A month later, I heard from Kevin that Mike was in the same youth detention centre as Kevin's younger brother. At least he was safe.

The house we rented was close to my sister, and Alexis accompanied her cousins Tom and Katy to a tiny village school at Charsfield. We bought a high-top Volkswagen van and I usually drove them all to school along roads so narrow that two cars couldn't pass. Tom and Katy loved the van's extra height; they could see over the hedgerows and discovered new views on their familiar journey to school.

Living in a different country, and not having the boys to worry about, distracted us for a while. Louise and I ventured out each day along the narrow Suffolk roads to explore the sights and sounds of our new country life—farms, castles, and ancient buildings were tucked into the folds of the gently rolling Suffolk landscape.

Alexis enjoyed the new experience of having cousins close by and going to school with them in England, but wondered why they had beans on toast so much for school lunches. I told her it was tradition. She was getting experience of living in my home country—often a disconnect between immigrants and their children.

I got busy modifying the van for our trip to Europe by building extra roof storage, so Louise could bring back souvenirs, and installing an alarm system. We planned to leave on the first of January and head south to the warmer climate of the Algarve in Portugal.

We packed everything in the van, including Alexis' voluminous home-schooling books. It was a tight fit. We were used to a house. There was an upper sleeping compartment for Alexis, and the settee below converted into a bed for Louise and me. Our new tiny home had a sink, gas stove, fridge, toilet, dining table, and curtains for privacy.

We left my sister's village on the first of January after watching the traditional New-Year's-Day foxhunt depart from the village. It made a grand sight—thirty horse-riders in red jackets pounding down the lane, jumping over hedges with the hunting horns blaring and dogs barking in full pursuit—grand, unless you were the fox. As the excitement drained from the air, we started the engine and wound our way through the misty Suffolk lanes onto the A23 and down to London.

We visited Madame Tussaud's wax museum, the Tower of London, and St Paul's Cathedral, and then parked on the street to spend our first night in the van.

The temperature was unusually cold. We were freezing and ran the propane heater all night, until it stopped around 6 a.m. It must have run the battery flat—not a great beginning to our trip. I had jumper cables and shook them at passing cars until someone finally stopped to let me use his car to jump-start the van. With the engine running, we turned the heater up full blast, made some tea, singed some bread on the gas grill, and had beans on toast for breakfast.

We drove south to the port of Newhaven, my former hometown, and stopped overnight at my Mum's before catching the ferry to Dieppe the next day. After a hearty breakfast of bacon and eggs, we hugged Mum goodbye, piled back into the van, and drove the mile onto the car ferry to start our adventure in Europe.

On reaching Dieppe, we gingerly drove off the ferry on the wrong side of the road, and headed towards Paris. Because the steering wheel was on the right and we drove on the right side of the road, I had to wait for an all-clear from Louise before I pulled out to overtake slower vehicles. As we drove the 190 kilometres to Paris, the temperature dipped below freezing. We parked the van on crunchy gravel in the Bois de Boulogne campsite. Using our van supplies, we had beans on toast and soup, turned the heater on, and went to bed.

Over the next few days we dressed warmly and filled our eyes with the sights in the Louvre, the Eiffel Tower, and the palace of Versailles. Usually, we got a cab into Paris, but on returning, our little van heater struggled to keep us warm. The temperature dropped to minus six Celsius. After three chilly nights, we'd had enough of being cold, bid Paris adieu and departed towards the warmer weather of Spain.

We were entranced by the breath-taking mountain beauty of Galicia, adjusted to the simplicity of life in the van, and met fellow adventurers seeking the escape of road-roaming through Europe. While I drove through Spain, Louise and Alexis did home-schooling exercises. I could tell that the tuition was a little rocky as they both adapted to their new teacher-student relationship.

My dreams of a year's adventure together ended in Portugal. After six weeks on the road and six weeks camped by the warm beaches of the Algarve, Louise became concerned about her father's health and Mike being alone. I was concerned about her dad too. He had just started suffering some arrhythmia but was responding well to medication. Regarding Mike, of course I was worried, but after years of being subjected to my sons' shenanigans, trying to help, understand, and do the right thing as a parent, I no longer wanted to change my plans for them.

LOUISE, ALEXIS AND ROD CAMPING IN THE ALGARVE, PORTUGAL

Louise was more of a homebody. We had been away over six months and she was missing the house, her parents, and friends. It was different for me. Home meant work, and work meant solving people's boat problems. I was a problem-solver, but by golly, it was nice to have break, especially as I had reached forty-four. Dad never got a break. For once, I wanted to look after myself and not be persuaded to curtail the trip or break the agreement with Kevin or the people who had rented our house.

After much discussion, each of us trying to get the other to change their position, we amicably, but sadly, decided to part company. I drove north to Lisbon's Portela Airport, gave them each a long hug, and watched them walk into the airport.

I started the van, threaded my way out of Lisbon without my co-navigator, and headed toward Madrid. The work of driving—watching for road signs, passing slower vehicles and shifting gears, felt like life on the road as normal, but the joy of pointing out new sights to one another was over.

I navigated through the day humming to Enya tapes, reached the evening, drove late into night, and almost crashed the van as my eyes fluttered with fatigue at 2 a.m.

I pulled off the highway onto a quiet side street and turned off the engine. Complete silence settled into the van—the silence of one heart beating. I put my elbows on the wheel, my face in my hands and sat alone in the silence of the black Spanish night. My body started to convulse. Warm tears ran down my arms and onto my jeans.

Being on holiday alone hadn't been part of the plan. Maybe I had been pig-headed to carry on by myself. At home, I was a father, husband, and neighbour—at work a busy businessman. I didn't know how to be alone. I lay down on my side, tucked my knees up and pulled a quilt over myself.

The sun woke me a few hours later, streaming through the unclosed curtains—Louise had always drawn them at night. My wife and daughter's voices no longer filled the air; the cupboards were empty of their clothes. Their bodies no longer shared the space. The only movements jostling the parked van were my own. My escape vehicle had become solitary confinement.

I had a cup of tea and some chocolate, then some more chocolate, and sat for a long time.

I could do this. Rinsing the cup and throwing the chocolate wrapper into the garbage, I climbed back into the driver's seat, consulted the map, started the engine and headed east, humming along with Enya's *"Sail Away."*

Not up for exploring a city on my own, I continued past Madrid toward Alicante, where my friends Rick and Ann had a bar and horse stable. They were pleased to see a fellow ex-pat. Ann cooked wonderful meals, while Rick introduced me to Spanish brandy and showed me how to ride a horse—both new experiences—one seemed to compliment the other. The brandy took away the fear of riding horses, and my friends' hospitality buoyed up my spirits. Four days later, with some equilibrium restored, I resumed my position in the driver's seat, said a fond farewell to Rick and Anne, and headed for Italy.

To keep in touch with my other life, I bought phone cards to check in with Louise and Kevin every week, or when possible. Alexis was glad to be back with her school friends. Louise's father was taking medication for his arrhythmia and was doing well. The Nissan Outboard sales were doing fine, and there was enough work for the mechanic. Mike was back living at home, but on probation. Everyone was doing well without me.

My journey took me to another seven countries. Sometimes I picked up hitchhikers for company, or chatted to fellow travellers in campgrounds—a great way to learn about which sights to visit. I was awestruck by the impressive ruins in Pompeii, Italy, frozen in time under the ominous shadow of the petulant Mount Vesuvius. I was stunned as the amazing mountain-top monasteries of Meteora, in Greece, burst across the windshield. I got drunk in a bar in Athens and for company, hired a female guide to take me around the Acropolis. She wore a jaunty hat, talked non-stop, and got annoyed when I asked her questions about things she had already explained.

Nearing the Turkish border, I stopped to pick up a young man hitchhiking.

"Do you speak English?" he asked.

"All the time," I replied.

"Are you driving to Turkey?"

"Yes."

"I can come?"

"Yes."

I opened the side door and Niko put his backpack in the van. We glanced at each other warily, hoping for the best but prepared for the worst. We didn't speak much at first. Niko was a twenty-one-year-old student from Slovenia, taking a break from university.

As we tried to leave Greece, the immigration official became angry. "You have wrong stamp in passport. You cannot leave Greece. Stamp is wrong."

"Look, you immigration guys do the stamps, not me." We argued back and forth. "Am I supposed to live here the rest of my life because one of you officials got the stamp wrong? That's ridiculous."

He scowled at me, stamped my passport, and we drove the hundred yards to the Turkish border. The Turkish immigration official said I didn't have the right insurance papers for the van and refused me entry.

"Get back in line, look sad, say sorry, keep going back. After time, he will be tired and let you pass," said Niko.

What did this kid know?

"Why do you think that?"

"I am from communist country. I am experience of bureaucrats."

Niko's suggestion seemed better than going back and arguing with the Greek immigration guy already unhappy with me. After the third time in the long line, two hours later, the Turkish official let me through after paying a small fine. He showed his disdain by pushing my documents off the counter onto the floor, but pointed to the door. I was in!

We explored Turkey together, visiting the Egyptian Bazaar and Blue Mosque in Istanbul, the killing fields of Gallipoli, a Turkish bath in Izmir, and the blue Roman bathing pools set in white limestone at Pamukkale. Two weeks after we met, we parted ways at a lonely fork in the road. Niko continued hitchhiking on to Pakistan, and I was catching the ferry to Greece. He had been a great companion. Much later, he became the general manager for Opel cars Hungary. We are still in touch.

On my return journey towards England, at Niko's suggestion, I stayed with his brother, Tomaz, in Ljubljana, and slept in Niko's bed. Tomaz took me to his uncle's beach-house in Croatia, and on another day, escorted me through the beautiful limestone caverns in Postojna, Slovenia. It was great to have friendly company.

After Louise and Alexis left, I tried to meet people en route, to help stave off the loneliness. But most of the time I planned, navigated, drove, slept, and ate by myself. Sometimes I didn't speak to anyone for days, which made me feel hollow inside, empty—a person with a hole for a centre.

In Italy I had my wallet stolen and suffered pain from kidney stones, which subsided after about a week. In Greece, I navigated to cities I couldn't pronounce because of their strange alphabet. In Ljubljana, the public phones didn't take Slovenian money—people used tokens instead. In Prague, I sat alone at the bar, had two beers and asked in English, Italian, and French how much the bill was. No one understood. I guessed at the cost, put some money on the counter, and left.

Most of my visits to bars were no longer than the time it took to drink two beers. I never felt comfortable too far from the van in case I couldn't find my way back, or it got broken into.

In my work at the shop, I made the cascade of daily decisions alone, but at four o'clock, I went home to a familiar house, people, TV, and language. My solo van travels were the kind of alone that didn't stop at the end of the day. Alone, was always there, a silent, pervasive companion. I thought things instead of saying them, remembered things to tell someone later, cooked my own meals, and visited tourist sites with unshared appreciation. I learned how to be alone. I learned the value of company.

After twelve months away, I crossed the channel from Holland to England, sold the van to a dealer, and caught the plane back to Vancouver—back to my familiar life.

26 - Back to Vancouver Forward with Stirling

*"The most important thing is to sacrifice what you are now
for what you can become tomorrow."*
— Shannon L. Alder

It felt good to be back home with friends, family, and the familiar patterns of everyday life instead of being a constant stranger. There were a few changes.

Louise had taken over making sure the doors were locked at night, taking out the garbage, opening the bills and paying them, and making sure the dog had been out.

We were a little wary of one another—Louise in case I was upset at her for *not* staying to finish the trip, and me in case she was mad at me *for* staying. It was the first time we had been apart in twenty-three years of marriage, and it was vaguely worrying that we had managed so well. Louise had negotiated with the school so that Alexis wouldn't miss a grade, providing she did some catch-up work. Mike and Steve were around, but not living at home.

Jet lag robbed me of sleep, and, curious to visit the shop, I left my favourite Turkish silk shirt in the closet, donned my work clothes, and drove the familiar twenty-minute route to work at 7 a.m.

Unlocking the door, I walked into the dusty shop and was happy to see there were four boats under repair. Good, we had work. Kevin had vacuumed the office carpet, and my fourteen-drawer oak desk looked clean and tidy—only the phone, fax and calculator sat on its broad surface. The familiar odour of polyester resin hung in the air as I lowered myself into the black swivel seat and looked out at the corrugated iron building across the street. I forgot we had put bars across the window after the robbery.

The metal building across the street was certainly a change from the stream of exotic landscapes sliding past the van's windshield. I leaned back in the chair. My eyes fluttered closed. The minarets of Istanbul appeared. Niko and I were wandering through the Egyptian Bazaar, sampling tasty Turkish food.

Ring, ring—the bars on the window reappeared as I jumped

217

awake and fumbled for the phone.

"General Boatworks."

"Hi, Graham Smith here. You repaired our twenty-four-foot Starcraft three or four years ago but it started leaking again. Is it covered on warranty?"

"No, I'm afraid not. If you look at your invoice, you'll see riveted aluminum boats are only covered for one year."

"We wanted to use it this weekend, but my wife worries when the bilge pump goes on all the time. Can I bring it in?" Dances with customers had resumed.

At 7.30 a.m. the lads arrived to start work; it was handshakes and laughter as we sat in the lunchroom having coffee together for the first time in a year. The crew consisted of Kevin, Bob, John, Rob, and Steve, the mechanic—all my regular guys. Good, we were already slimmed down for the fall. There would be no need to lay anyone off.

I spent an hour and a half with Kevin, bringing me up to speed on everything. No major problems, except that a court case had been delayed. Darn, I was hoping Kevin would handle that. There had been a few minor mishaps, but generally he had managed very well. I calculated that the company had made a small profit of $5,000, which I turned over to Kevin as per our agreement.

I think he felt a little strange stepping back from the role of running the business just as he was getting the hang of being in charge. I never knew what he was thinking or feeling. In the business world feelings weren't discussed, just results. Nonetheless, I did somehow feel protective of him; he was about the same age as my sons and his father had died in a car accident just before he came to work for me.

Being alone in the van made me realize that I was on my own at work. I taught Alexis to answer the phone, but she was only nine and it would be a while before she could help. My wife and kids lived separate lives, not part of my work, except Louise cleaned our washroom once a week.

Speaking of kids, Steve had been active while I was away. He got a job as a vacuum cleaner salesman. After selling one vacuum cleaner, he talked a car salesman into selling him a brand new Mustang.

Three weeks after buying the car, he had a head-on collision on the Sea to Sky highway and totalled his new vehicle. The police said it was one of the first cars equipped with air bags and that they had probably saved his life, thank God!

Although I slipped easily back into the business world and was glad to see my customers, subcontractors and workers, the urgency of survival was missing. The house and shop were paid for; nothing pulled me forward across new frontiers. If I could take a year off, things must be running well.

Survival, and the creation of a safe economic harbour for the family, had been my driving force. I had assumed that not being driven by necessity would be a good thing, but it made work less meaningful. Once the soccer coaching was through and I quit racing dirt bikes, there was little challenge except for the weekly badminton in the winter. Strange what a trip away can bring into your head. With the mortgages paid, I should have felt happy, but instead, there was less sense of purpose. I coasted along in cruise for a year or so, until I met Darryl.

Darryl had a twenty-five-foot Bertram. He had run into some rocks and tried to repair the damage himself, following advice from friends, by laminating the outside with epoxy, but it still leaked. I estimated the boat in Burnaby as it sat on his trailer parked on the street.

"Darryl, you should get your boat off the street. Someone could easily break in and steal the electronics, or even the whole boat. There's no security on the street."

"I can't afford to pay for any repairs for another two weeks till I get paid."

"Bring it into the shop now and pay me in two weeks' time. At least it will be safe."

Darryl appreciated my offer and took me out for lunch. Instead of having a relaxed meal, he kept telling me about his men's group, how it had helped him to be the man he had "always wanted to be." I listened out of politeness. He explained how men struggle alone without a network, whereas women did networks better and talked about their problems instead of storing them inside.

I declined. "I'm not much of a group person, and to be honest, it sounds kinda weird—no offence."

"That's exactly what I said, but I went to a meeting, joined the group and it's been really great."

The "really great" description worried me. Too much like a sales pitch. "Not right now, Darryl, but thanks anyway. "

"Rod, come to one meeting. That's all I ask. Then I'll never mention it again."

"Where is it?"

"Norgate Park, 7 p.m. this Friday. I'll pick you up."

"No, thanks. I'll get there under my own steam." If I went, I wanted to ensure my escape by having my own car.

The meeting was held in a small corrugated iron shed by the football field. There were twelve guys there—four guests and eight initiates. They started off by playing a game of "no-rules rugby," except the ball was a two-foot-long horse thighbone. At one point, there were four guys pulling on it at once. It was kind of a rough-and-ready camaraderie, but fun. Puffed out, we adjourned to the enrolment meeting.

Eventually, after a lot of cajoling and persuasion and hearing once again about all the wondrous benefits, I signed up for the Stirling Men's Weekend. Sneakily, no one would tell me what took place there, but all the "Stirling Men" told stories of personal growth and better relationships with their wives and kids. That's how I came to join the Stirling Institute of Relationships. I didn't buy a lot of the BS they were peddling, but the men's weekend turned out to be a meaningful bonding event.

There were 200 of us in what looked like some kind of army barracks, fifty miles south of the border, in Washington State. After some initial distrust, I began to engage in the spirit of the weekend.

Justin Stirling, a charismatic, controversial guy, led us in exercises designed to peel away the bullshit and reveal our true selves. We were all sworn to secrecy. I got up my courage and led the grieving section by talking about my father's death when I was eighteen. It was the first time I had talked about it to anyone. It felt good after—like a burden had been lifted. After two full days of bonding, the last section of the weekend was a celebration of our manhood. We were somehow imbued with the energy of 200 male brothers, which left us feeling connected, enriched, and powerful—for a while.

After the men's weekend, we were put on teams to keep the spirit of the men's weekend alive. There were six people on my team, and we met weekly in my outboard showroom.

Men talked about their challenges and their feelings. It was intriguing to hear. No way I was going to share my inner feelings— they were private—but after three months of listening to other men sharing, I started talking about my feelings. It felt weird and risky, but also cleansing. It wasn't easy. Sometimes men trailed off into a "story" and were promptly brought back.

"Don't start bullshitting us again. How are you feeling?" When you have six guys telling you something, it doesn't make sense to say, "You're all wrong." The team was like a conscience, helping to guide one another in the right direction. I came out of the weekly meetings empowered and energized by my new support team. I was getting help with my life and helping others with theirs.

MY STIRLING MEN'S TEAM

I became a believer, and took on the new challenge of getting other guys to do the men's weekend so that they could have a community of supportive men in their lives. I got more hugs in the two years I was on the team than in most of my previous life. I let other Stirling Men's teams use my showroom for meetings and gave Stirling Men priority if they needed their boats repaired.

George Halima was one such case. He was a wiry guy of about forty, and an avid sailor. He needed his thirty-foot C & C sailboat repaired in time to compete in the Swiftsure race in Victoria. He had placed well in the previous year and was excited about going in again. George really needed his yacht by Friday. He had paid his entry fee, then his *Atomic 4* engine had quit, and, unable to stop, he had run into a cement dock. We had to repair his bow and his engine. He didn't have a girlfriend and spent every spare minute on this boat. Being a postman, if he was fast on his route, he could finish early and go sailing every day.

Returning from Powell River, he had recently taken on some bad gas and now had water in his fuel tank, which had caused the problem.

Engines just won't run on water! My neighbour's 16-year-old son, Danny, was working for us at the time. He was of Ukrainian descent but sported a huge afro.

"Danny, I am going to run water through this hose up into the fuel tank of the boat. When the hose is full, we'll turn the tap off, unscrew the hose, and let the contents of the tank syphon into the lane."

I explained that clear water would come out first and when it switched from clear colour to the purple of marine gas, he was to immediately put the hose into the adjacent 45-gallon drum. The fluid trickled out quite slowly. Danny got distracted and started doing something else. About fifteen gallons of gas was released into the lane, which was an explosion hazard. Someone reported us.

The fire department came down and we got fined. The *North Shore News* reported us and took a picture of the offending lane under the headline, "Local boat yard caught dumping gas in lane." No one mentioned that I had given a high school student a summer job.

We raced to remove all the woodwork from above the affected fuel tank, pulled it out, power washed the tank, rinsed the inside with a gallon of methyl hydrate to absorb any remaining water, then reinstalled it and replaced the flooring. We put five gallons of gas in the tank, ran the engine in the shop to make sure everything worked, and then pleaded with Bob the boat mover, to take the boat to Lynwood Marina for launching right away.

George was beside himself with joy. We had dropped everything to get him launched by Friday. It was always rewarding to help boaters achieve their plans, especially another Stirling man. George was super-pleased and dropped off a case of beer for my guys on Thursday at quitting time. Danny wasn't allowed to have any. I could imagine a new *North Shore News* headline, "Local boat yard caught giving beer to teen."

George phoned later in the day sounding panicky.

"Rod, I've got another problem. I just found my mast light doesn't work. I gotta have it working for the race."

"Leave it with me. I'll get back to you." I phoned Stewart, the mast guy at Pro-tech.

"Rod, I'm swamped. Can't do anything for at least three days."

"But this guy is a buddy of mine and he's all booked to go into the Swiftsure."

"I've got three customers going in the Swiftsure. That's why we're swamped. Sorry."

I phoned Mosquito Creek and Race Rocks marinas to see if we could use either of their mast towers, a specialised raised platform sticking out from the dock, to fix George's light, but they were fully booked. Time was running out. I had an idea: If we brought the sailboat close to the road, maybe one of my guys could sit in a bosun's chair and a HIAB, a truck with a hydraulic arm, could lift him up to the mast to replace the light. Yes!

I phoned my usual HIAB company. Yes, they had a truck available at 2 p.m. No, they would not lift a person in a bosun's chair up to a sailboat mast. They were not insured to lift people, only objects. The next two companies said the same thing.

Damn—time to phone the owner. "George, I can't get anyone to fix the light. I tried everybody."

Silence—I could imagine him slumping. I didn't like silences. George may have known that.

"Do you have a halyard going through the top of the mast?" I asked. "If you do, maybe I could get one of my guys to go up in a bosun's chair and fix the light."

"That would be amazing, Rod. I don't think I'm allowed in the race unless everything is shipshape."

I thought Rob might do it. He was twenty-one and kind of wild. At sixteen-years-old, he had gone to live with his dad in Australia, but then left to become a freelance rodeo rider. He had part of his finger missing where a bull had crushed his hand against the fence. I thought going up a mast should be easy for him. I talked him into coming down to look at the boat. I took a light bulb and a bosun's chair I'd made of plywood to the marina. The mast of the *C & C 30* is about thirty feet high. It doesn't look bad when you are at the bottom looking up.

George was right; there was a halyard made of nylon braid running through a pulley at the top of the mast. I guessed the three-eighths-inch braid was good for at least 600 pounds of weight.

"Plenty strong enough for your weight, Rob, and a lot easier ride than a rodeo bull, eh?" Rob didn't reply and looked away.

I fastened the halyard onto the bosun's chair sling using a double sheet bend and held it while Rob got in. "We'll both pull on the rope together, Rob. Our combined weight should move you up there fine." He remained silent. "Okay, together—pull, pull, pull."

He went up a foot at a time. At about twelve feet, he stopped pulling. "I gotta come down. Get me down, *get me down!*" His whole body shook.

"Okay, okay, relax. I'll hook the halyard under this cleat and lower you down."

Rob reached the deck. He was panicked, teary, and breathing fast.

"What's up, Rob? You look in bad shape."

"Yeah. I fell off a ladder once when I was about five. Never been up a ladder since. I thought sittin' in the chair would be okay, but it fuckin' wasn't. Jesus, I feel like puking."

I went into my Stirling mode and gave him a hug. "Take some deep breaths, Rob. You're down now. You're gonna be okay."

"Yeah, thanks, man. Thanks."

"I thought you'd be okay after riding rodeo bulls."

"Yeah, well them bulls was only six feet off the ground."

"I'd be scared shitless to ride a bull, but I have been up a few masts when I was in the Merchant Navy." It felt good to brag a little.

"Why don't you go up then, Rod? I'll help pull you."

I was twenty-seven years older than Rob. Here was a chance to show the kid how it was done, but I didn't want to do it. I didn't like heights. He was looking at me. Male bravado took over. I sat in the chair.

"We can try. Not sure if the two of us can pull me up. I'm heavier than you. We'll just see if it works, but I probably won't do it right now. There's a couple of things at the shop I need to do." Saying no flat out seemed too chicken. Everyone has their pride—even 48-year-old guys.

"You used to be in the Navy, didn't you, Rod? You must have gone up the mast then."

"Yeah, I did—twenty-eight years ago."

I sat in the chair and we both pulled. I went up surprisingly easily. We pulled in unison hand over hand, me on the chair and Rob on the deck. I was already halfway up. It had been easier than I thought. Maybe I should just keep going, get the job done.

"It's going good, Rob. Let's take a break. See that cleat at the bottom of the mast? Wrap the rope around it in a figure eight." I looked down to see if he was doing it right and was shocked to see how far it was down to the deck. A wave of panic went through me. I took some deep breaths. I remembered feeling like this at sea—panicky and shaky about heights.

"You okay?" yelled Rob.

"Yeah, just getting my breath."

He walked over to the side of the deck to spit. The boat rocked and I swung about three feet to starboard and slowly back. "Don't walk around Rob, it rocks the boat."

"Okay. Shall we get pulling again?" said Rob.

My heart had slowed a little. What could go wrong?

"Okay."

I went up a foot at a time as we both steadily pulled on the halyard. I stared straight ahead at the mast. My arms were aching, but I kept pulling, and finally, I reached the top.

"Tie the rope around the cleat like you did last time, Rob." I didn't look down.

"Okay. Wow, you are up there, man!"

The noise from the bridge traffic above the marina seemed louder. I could just reach the light. It was tough to unscrew. A boat motored past us and my weight at the top of the mast increased the rolling movement. The mast described big arcs across the sky. I glanced

226

down and froze. Wrapping both arms around the mast, I closed my eyes and waited for the rocking to stop. I might as well have been hanging from the top of the Empire State Building. Both meant death if I fell. The Empire State building might have been better. It didn't move.

"Hurry up. I gotta go soon."

"What do you mean, you gotta go soon?" I yelled down. "You never told me that."

"You never asked. I just thought we were coming to look at something."

Damn Rob—so unreliable. I kept my left hand wrapped around the mast while my right crept up to the light again. I torqued the clear plastic light cover with all my remaining strength. It came loose. I unscrewed the cover, held it in my mouth, exchanged the bulbs and screwed the cover back in place.

Pulling myself aloft and clinging to the mast, the tension of being almost thirty feet above the deck and the mast's wild swings had syphoned off my energy.

"Okay, Rob, start letting me down slowly."

"Hand over hand like going up?"

"No. Don't have the strength. Keep tension on the rope, run it under the cleat at the base of the mast and pay it out slowly like I did for you."

"What?"

I repeated the instructions, but held tight to the rope just in case Rob got it wrong. He didn't, and I began to descend. Good—the light was fixed and I was safely on my way down. Mission accomplished. Eighteen feet above the deck, there was a faint click and I stopped descending.

"Keep paying out the rope, Rob."

"I am, man. Its loose."

"Loose? It can't be. I stopped coming down."

"I'm tellin' you, it's fuckin' loose. Loose as a goose."

I was feeling pretty loose myself. "Okay, let's try pulling me up, see if we can un-budge it."

We both heaved to no avail; the rope was stuck fast. Damn. Somehow it had become jammed in the sheave at the top of the mast. Maybe my weight had been too much for the small pulley and it had broken.

"Like I said, I gotta go. Got a dentist appointment in fifteen minutes. But I'll stop by the shop and tell Kevin to come down right away."

"Jeez, Rob, I'm stuck here. Make sure Kev comes right away."

Even when Kevin came, I would still be stuck. I suddenly realized that Rob had not tied the end of the halyard around the cleat at the base of the mast. If the halyard suddenly freed itself I would plummet down to the deck. I grabbed the loose end of the halyard and wound it three times around my right foot. I kept my leg straight to keep pressure on the halyard, in case it became unstuck.

Five uncomfortable minutes passed, then ten. Dangling from the mast was damned uncomfortable. My brain started formulating an escape. I would unwind the halyard from my foot, cut it, tie one end around the mast above my head, and use it to lower myself down.

How could I cut the halyard? There was a tiny penknife on my car keys. I needed to do this quickly. The halyard holding me might come unstuck and drop me eighteen feet onto the deck.

I unwound the halyard from my foot, placed the halyard against the mast, and started sawing through with the tiny knife. The blade was dull. After three minutes of frantic slicing, it finally cut through. With fatigued arms, I took the halyard and tied it to the mast above my head then looped the line through the bosun's chair sling to make the lowering hitch I had learned in sea school.

Now to cut the halyard supporting me: I gripped the miniscule knife again, and with numb fingers started sawing through. Another boat went by and rocked the mast. I stopped, clung on to the mast with both arms, then resumed. My arm was aching, but I was getting close. I wrapped my legs around the mast until the new halyard took up the slack. The braid parted with a little ripping noise and I slid gently down the mast until the new line supported my weight.

The lowering hitch worked, but barely. I had to keep my legs wrapped around the mast to take some of the pressure off so the hitch wouldn't jam. Luckily, the plywood seat was a foot wide so the mast scraped against the plywood instead of my genitals. I was exhausted and could hardly keep my arms above my head to force the braid into the lowering hitch. Ten-feet gone, eight to go, descending two-inches at a time. I rested for a few minutes, and summoning the very last of my strength, lowered myself onto the deck. I stepped shakily out of the bosun's chair and crumpled into a foetal position on the deck, exhausted, but relieved to have made it down alive.

A patter of footsteps approached the sailboat.

"Hey, what's up? Takin' a break?" asked Kevin. "Rob said you wanted me."

"I was stuck halfway up the damned mast and had to get myself down. What the heck took you so long?"

"I was getting some parts," Kevin explained. "When I got back, Bob told me Rob dropped by and said to come to George's boat right away. So here I am."

I explained to Kevin the details of my journey down the mast and then left for the day. I stopped at the Lynwood and had a couple of beers with Trevor. He was impressed with my escape from certain death—well, possible death, but certain injury. The mast had got a little higher by the second beer.

I lay in bed that night pondering my day.

Had I gone up just to look good in front of Rob? Was it stupidity or courage?

Either way, my workers were impressed and the customer was happy, but I was never going up another mast, ever. The event went unmentioned to Louise. She would have been alarmed and would have no difficulty deciding if it was courageous or stupid.

I met with my men's group the next evening. We sat among the outboard motors, drank coffee and checked in with one another. Meetings were usually two hours long. They appreciated the warrior aspect of my mast story and I got a few cheers and back slaps.

"Right on, Rod," said Diamond. "That was some scary shit. You got out of it well."

"Sounds to me like maybe you went up there because you're bored," said Mike.

"I was taking care of business. The guy just needed his light fixed."

"You risked your life for that? To me, you're not enthused about your business lately. You would only take a risk like that if you were bored."

"You don't like your work much either." I hit back at Mike, not wanting to listen.

"You're right, but I don't have choices and you do. Your house and warehouse are paid for. How's your bottom line? Are you making money?" Mike was about my age, intense, and an accountant.

"Right now, I guess we're doing a little better than breaking even," I said.

"Jeez, you've been running the shop all these years, handling all the hassle, breathing resin fumes and fibreglass dust just to break even?"

"Yeah, I know—maybe you're right. I'm not fired up like I used to be, but what am I gonna do—just quit?"

"Find something you like, then quit. Sell the business, keep the warehouse, live on the rent till you establish yourself in another field." Murmurs of approval echoed around the team.

Mike's idea would mean a huge change in my life. I felt like saying, "You're all wrong," except maybe they weren't. "I don't know what I like—never thought about it. I've just been doing this to earn a living."

"Maybe go and talk to Aron Prinz, the counsellor—help you figure shit out. He's helped a lot of Stirling Men," said Mike.

I respected Mike; he'd played professional football for the CFL and been on the Olympic luge team. All the team had my respect. They were all accomplished men.

"I had a buddy went to him, said he was pretty good," agreed Glen.

More murmurs of agreement and nodding heads from my team.

"Here's his number," said Mike. "Give it a try, Baker."

I passed the coffee round and we moved on to the topic of enrolling more men into the Stirling Men's Weekend.

27 - At the End There Was a Beginning
*"You are never too old to set another goal
or to dream a new dream."*
— C. S. Lewis

It was 9 p.m. and the hustle of downtown Vancouver had slowed as darkness descended. I parked my car and took the elevator up to the sixteenth floor of the high-rise on Georgia Street, where Aron's office was located. I rapped on the door and waited, running on trust from my team and thinking about what to say. It didn't seem like a counselling session—two guys meeting at night in a downtown office. A white-haired man opened the door and welcomed me with a warm smile and a firm handshake. There was something about him that was trustworthy. I couldn't decide what.

"Come in, Rod, come in. Glad you could make it in the evening and accommodate my schedule."

Aron explained that this was his office, where he worked as a handwriting analyst for businesses. He could tell a person's character by their handwriting.

I became nervous. "Are you going to test mine?"

My handwriting was awful.

"Maybe later, but first sit down, Rod, and tell me how I can be of help." We sat facing each other in black leather chairs.

"My men's team suggested I visit you. I guess I'm feeling a bit lost."

"A bit lost?"

"For the last nineteen years, I've run my own boat repair company. I started it when I was out of work to support my family, but I guess I've accomplished what I set out to do."

I explained that while helping people with their boats was rewarding, the day-to-day business was a hassle. I had stress from two sons who kept getting into trouble and a marriage which wasn't as close as it used to be.

"I kind of thought my family would pitch in and help with the business, but they haven't. Now the mortgage is paid and we own the

233

building, maybe… I don't know." It seemed selfish to talk about myself—about what I wanted.

"Maybe you would like to do something different?" suggested Aron.

"Yeah, but it would be tough because the boat business is all I know. Plus, having worked for myself all these years, it might be difficult to work for someone else."

"Seems to me, Rod, you didn't know anything about boat repairs when you started, but you had a great incentive to learn, is that right?"

"Yeah, that's right," I chuckled.

"So, if you found something you *might* like, given your track record, you might have that same energy to invest in learning something new?"

"Yeah, maybe."

It seemed logical, but he was making it all sound too easy. For one thing, I couldn't think what line of work would interest me.

As though reading my mind, Aron passed me a career aptitude test. "Take ten minutes, Rod, fill this in and we'll take a look—get something figured out."

I set aside my doubts and started filling in the multi-page form. Aron made it seem the natural thing to do, and did some paperwork while I wrote. It took fifteen minutes. Most of the answers just needed ticks. Aron wouldn't see my handwriting.

He perused the form for a few minutes and smiled. "Well, Rod, you hit all tens on one career."

"Ten out of a hundred?"

"You hit ten out of ten on every measure for being a counsellor."

His words rolled into me and filled me up. It was a warm feeling. Ten out of ten for being a counsellor sounded good—encouraging. Jim, a former employee, had taken a similar career aptitude test after getting injured at work and found his strongest career option was "rabbit breeder." Counsellor sounded better, kind of fatherly, knowledgeable, and helpful.

Yes, I could see myself in that role. I felt a surge of excitement.

Aron made things seem possible.

"Okay, sounds good. What should happen next?"

"Write your signature for me, Rod."

I did my usual squiggle, which had been corrupted into something illegible after so many years of signing thousands of business cheques.

"Could you write it so that I could read it, Rod?"

I tried again.

"Still can't read *Rodney Baker*. Keep trying."

On my fourth attempt, I arrived at something Aron approved of.

"Good, Rod, good. Now, I have something else for you to consider. The way you are dressed—it doesn't represent the man in front of me."

"I have been dressing rougher since I joined Stirling, that's why I'm wearing jeans and a T-shirt now. I got the message it was the man who mattered, not the clothes *on* the man."

"I understand that, Rod. Sounds like you changed to align yourself with Stirling. As you are here, I'm guessing you might be up for some more change. Is that correct?"

"Yeah, I guess so." We both laughed.

"Here are some ideas for you to consider. I would like you to write your signature 2,000 times, but legibly like you just did. You can come back and give them to me in two weeks. I would like you to think about dressing in a way that better represents who you are— your person, your character, *you*. You might not understand why I am suggesting these changes, so try acting on both these suggestions as an act of faith."

"I'm not much on faith, Aron."

"Fair enough. How about you try these changes as an experiment?"

I had no idea why, but I trusted Aron. He was compelling without being pushy, and it was exciting to have someone believe in me.

"Yeah, okay, I will try."

"How did it feel to hear that you scored top marks for being a counsellor?"

"It felt good, surprising, and good. But I am not sure what to do next."

"What do you do at work when you need help with something outside your knowledge?"

"Look in the Yellow Pages."

"So, it would be normal for you to look in the Yellow Pages for a counselling school?"

"If you put it that way, yes, it would be." Wow, things were moving along fast. I already had some new ideas about what to do and how to put them into action.

"One last thing, Rod. If you are up for it, I would like us to pray to Saint Jude together."

If Aron had said this at the beginning, I would have probably walked out. I wasn't religious.

"Who is Saint Jude?"

"He is the patron saint of hope."

Ha, I would need hope to change careers at age 47.

"Okay, I'll try."

Aron dimmed the lights and took both my hands in his. They were soft and warm. I hadn't expected this—it's lucky I was flexible.

"Repeat after me: Oh, most holy apostle, Saint Jude, faithful servant and friend of Jesus, the Church honoureth and invoketh thee universally, as the patron of hopeless cases, and of things almost despaired of ..."

I heard my voice following Aron's. It was strange but familiar, risky but comforting. Something was flowing into me.

The next thing I remember, I found myself walking down the street in the cool night air, feeling lightheaded and carefree. I couldn't remember saying goodbye to Aron.

I got into my Nissan Micra, drove home, and started writing my name as Aron had instructed. The more I wrote my name, the better I felt—like I was creating something. Louise saw me writing in the bedroom and asked if I was writing an estimate. I said no, it was something else, some homework, writing my name. She looked

236

puzzled, but didn't comment. I wasn't sure what to say either.

I had a sudden urge to drive down to see my good friend Edouard, in Washington State, for the weekend. We had been best buddies until he moved down there for work two years ago. I told Louise that a break would do me good. She thought it was a little sudden, but she knew I missed Edouard.

I took off early Saturday morning and zoomed southward across the border toward Eddie's house. As I neared his house, in the tiny rural community of Horse Heaven Acres, the Yakima Police stopped me for speeding, but I somehow talked my way out of getting a ticket—unusual.

Edouard was happy to see me, but freaked out when I told him about my homework assignment of writing my name over and over, showing him the sheets of paper. He said I'd been brainwashed. I laughed, and replied, "Maybe washed, but not brainwashed." We always ribbed each other. We spent the day catching up. He told me about his new work in the food industry, and I explained about the Stirling Men's Weekend. Sabine, his wife, cooked us a tasty French meal that evening and he started ribbing me again at the dinner table.

"Sounds like a cult to me, Rod."

"You Frenchmen. Just because there are no women, you think it must be a cult."

"If he says it's good for him, why don't you stop criticising?" said Sabine. "Maybe having male friends would be good for you as well."

We set out the next morning for a hike, accompanied by Edouard's new border collie, Pele. Having hiked a fair distance over the treeless green hills, and thrown multiple sticks for the dog, we returned hungry to consume another *haute cuisine* dinner from Sabine.

We discussed the challenges my two *urbane* French friends had found living in "Horse Heaven Acres," deep in the Washington countryside. They had to drive miles to grocery store and they weren't used to farm country. Their neighbours had never met any Europeans and often gave them strange looks. The previous week, Sabine asked

Edouard where all the cows had gone in the fields surrounding their house. Upon checking with their neighbour, Dick, Edouard had learned they had been shipped to the slaughterhouse.

"They have killed them all," he'd explained to his wife.

"They have *killed* them all? Why have they killed them?" said a shocked Sabine. There were no beef cattle in Cannes.

Next morning at seven, Eddie got up to see me off. We drank a coffee together, he gave me a big hug, and we parted company. I jumped into the car and embarked upon the five-hour drive back to North Vancouver. I was full of energy and continued my writing homework when I got home.

Two thousand signatures is a tedious task, and it took time to replicate the nicely written signature I had written in Aron's office.

"Why are you writing your name over and over?" asked Louise. "You've never done anything like that before."

"This counsellor suggested it. The one I went to on Thursday."

"What's the point? It's looks creepy."

"I'm not actually sure, but it's supposed to help me. Oh yeah, something else—I am thinking of changing my work. I took an employment test and got ten out of ten for counsellor."

"Are you serious? What about General Boatworks? Don't you need qualifications to be a counsellor?"

"Yeah, I'm gonna find out about that. I'm thinking maybe I'll put the company up for sale."

"I'm not happy with that idea, Rod. How would we live?"

"When I started General Boatworks, you worried about me going into business—now you don't want me to sell it. We could live on the rent from the building, and the house is paid for. Both the boys have left and only Alexis is here, so there's less food to buy." I could see Louise getting concerned.

"Mike on my men's team is an accountant. He thinks it's a good idea."

"You've been acting weird ever since you've been on that men's team. I'm not sure its good for you."

Louise's voice was usually very soft—when strangers phoned the house, they often asked to speak to her father—but now her voice had become more strident. I tried a new tactic.

"You know how you said you didn't want to work in the office because it was too dusty and dirty? I'm beginning to feel the same way." Being the provider, I never spoke about my own needs concerning work. It was new territory.

I entered the shop on Monday, my first day back at work since seeing Aron. After doing the rounds and making sure my guys had work to do, I returned to my office and sat down at the fourteen-drawer oak desk I had built eighteen years previously. It had lasted well, except a corner of laminate was loose on the bottom right-hand drawer—just needed re-bonding with a dab of contact cement.

The fresh dawn light spilled through the barred office window as I talked boat repair business on the phone, but something new was happening. Between phone calls, I thumbed through the Yellow Pages. Most of the headings under counselling were counsellors advertising their practises, then I found the Counsellor Training Institute (CTI)—strange name. I didn't know what "Institute" meant, but the "Counsellor Training" sounded hopeful. I would phone them at nine o'clock. The more I thought about being a counsellor, the more I liked the idea.

Enrolling guys into the Stirling Men's Weekend felt like a counselling role by helping others to have supportive men in their lives. I got similar rewards from work. One of the best aspects about running General Boatworks was that I got to meet and help a lot of customers. It made me feel valuable. If I were a counsellor, I could cut out the boats and go straight to helping people with their life problems.

At forty-seven-years old, I'd seen a lot more life than the twenty-something therapist Louise and I had seen for marriage counselling. My father and my best friend both died when I was 18, so I knew about grief. While emigration had been a new beginning, I realized later, it was also about loss. Dealing with my sons' disruptive behaviour had provided insight into family problems, and as an entrepreneur, I also knew first-hand about business stress.

Years before, I had volunteered at the Vancouver Crisis Centre and enjoyed working with people in distress. I had quit the Crisis Centre when I started General Boatworks to have more time for business and family. It felt good to be heading back towards the helping field.

At nine o'clock, I carefully dialled the school's number.

"Counsellor Training Institute, Jean speaking. How can I help you?"

"Do you train counsellors at your facility?"

"Yes, we do. Would you like to come in to our office on Water Street for an orientation?"

"Maybe you could fax me a brochure first?"

"We don't usually do that, sir. It won't be in colour."

"Yes, I realize that. It's okay. My fax number is 980 6212. Thank you."

Jean was in no hurry; I got the brochure about an hour later. I could have driven there during that time. I laid both sheets of the brochure on my desk and studied them. One of the students featured in the brochure looked my age. I started reading: "*Courses are designed to provide adequate theoretical background knowledge of counselling and practical skill training, which can be immediately applied to counselling situations.*" The word "immediately" sounded good to me. I was starting this late in life and didn't want to wait around.

I made an appointment for an orientation, held every Friday. The classes ran in the morning from 8 a.m. till noon. I could attend counsellor training in the morning, then come back and run the shop in the afternoon. The course was one year long. I had been away from work for a year three years previously, so attending my business half-time for a year shouldn't be difficult.

Louise was concerned about the change. General Boatworks had supplied our income for most of our marriage. It was scary for me too, but the idea of becoming a counsellor pulled my head away from the boat business; it was a new calling—a new interest. I wanted to soak up everything there was to know about counselling, become knowledgeable, start my own practice, and help people with their life challenges rather than boat problems.

I told Kevin my plan to come in half-time and offered him a raise for the extra responsibility—twenty-one dollars an hour, the same wage I paid myself. He agreed, probably because he was able to resume some of the control and use the knowledge he had acquired in my year away.

I attended the counselling school orientation. The atmosphere was a little odd, but I put it down to counsellors trying to run a business. They seemed to make it difficult to take the course instead of easy. I signed up anyway; the course content seemed sound enough.

On my first day attending the Counsellor Training Institute, I parked and walked down the dock, treated myself to a cheese scone, and waited for the SeaBus. The school was located on Water Street, on the other side of Burrard Inlet. It felt very strange, entering a field of work based on my own choice rather than being driven by circumstantial needs. I hadn't done that since I found my first job as a rag baler at age sixteen. I chose that job because the work was close to my house, whereas this job was close to my heart. I felt a mix of exciting adventure and worrying self-indulgence.

For the next year, my mornings would not start by answering the phone, ordering parts or delegating work. Instead, I embarked upon a journey into the mind—my own, and that of others—an academic and emotional passage.

Excited and hopeful, I stepped aboard the SeaBus. It surged away from the dock, bearing me towards my new future as a counsellor.

Epilogue

A year later, on my last day of college, I boarded the SeaBus back to the North Shore a proud graduate of the Counsellor Training Institute.

On the first of October 1996, I sold my company and handed the keys of the shop to the new owner. It felt surreal. General Boatworks had been my life for twenty years, and now it was over. No more running for the phone, big cheques, the smell of fiberglass, or daily contact with my employees.

I drove to the beach in West Vancouver, sat on a log and stared out to sea for two hours, until dusk settled over the shoreline. After twenty-seven years, I was through working on boats.

You do a thing till it's over—then it's over.

An ocean breeze blew through my clothes and chilled me. I felt empty—like a wave thrown on the shore.

Counselling diploma in hand, I set out toward a new world. Like all travellers, I hoped there would be a place for me—a position where I could practice my new skills.

Two fellow graduates and I opened an office on Water Street. Our new counselling room was four floors up and had two windows overlooking the street. We painted the walls off-white, bought potted plants, put ads in the Yellow Pages, and a trickle of clients started to come to the office.

The problems of my clients affected me more deeply than those of my boat customers, but I tried not to get emotional, it stops the client talking if the therapist gets upset. It felt good to help people. My new direction had been right.

Unlike the boat business, some clients asked about my credentials. My diploma started to feel inadequate. It seemed that having a master's degree in counselling was the gold standard. I searched the internet for a University that would accept me without a B.A.

Life's journeys don't stop until life itself stops.

Acknowledgements

THE GENERAL BOATWORKS REPAIR TEAM CIRCA 1989

ROD JIM MARTIN BOB KEVIN JOHN

I am thankful to my employees, my family, my customers, and others, for providing the material, which forms the substance of this story.

Writing this book, my second, put me in touch with many wonderful beta readers who were generous with their time and helpful in their comments. Many thanks to Jessie Gussman, Julie Marksteiner, Elizabeth Watkins, Ross Hotchkiss, Trudi Luethy, Scott Skipper, Sonia Bellhouse, Maya Carlisle, Anna Adler, Neil Loewe, and Maggie Ulrich. My beta reader help was heart-warming proof that the kindness of strangers still exists in the world.

Thanks to my critique group, Barry, Kathy, and Doug for providing on-going support and encouragement.

Last, but not least, thanks to Anna, who continues to endure my nocturnal writing habits and nurture my writing creativity with her wonderful cooking.

About the Author

Rod Baker, MA, was born in England and, at age sixteen, joined the British merchant navy as a deck hand. He immigrated to Canada when he was twenty-one and worked as a tugboat mate, shipwright, businessman, psychotherapist, and CEO for mental health organizations. Rod lives in Lions Bay, BC.